The Architecture
of Persuasion

The Architecture
of Persuasion

How to Write Well-Constructed Sales Letters

Michael Masterson

AMERICAN WRITERS & ARTISTS INC.

For general information on our other products and services or for technical support, please contact our Member Services Department within the United States at (866) 879-2924, outside the United States at (561) 278-5557, or fax (561) 278-5929.

ISBN-13: 978-0-9821500-0-9
ISBN-10: 0-9821500-0-8

Printed in the United States of America

10 9 8 7 6 5 4 3 2 1

To Bill Bonner

Acknowledgements

Thanks to Katie Yeakle and the AWAI team for giving me a forum for preaching what I practice.

Thanks to Vicky Heron, Guillermo Rubio, Judy Strauss and Jill Perri for helping me pull it all together. And special thanks for the layout and design to Lorie Drozdenko of Crow Moon Marketing.

Thanks to Bill Bonner, Jay Abraham and Joel Nadel for my first important lessons in selling.

Thanks to all the copywriters I once taught who now regularly teach me: Don Mahoney, Paul Hollingshead, John Forde, Porter Stansberry, Mike Palmer, Steve Sjuggerud, Addison Wiggin, Jay Livingston, Charlie Byrne, Alexander Green, Justin Ford, Greg Grillot, Will Newman, Jennifer Stevens.

Foreword

Michael Masterson: The Architect of Copywriting

There are relatively few master copywriters. And there are even fewer great copywriting teachers. Michael Masterson is that rarest of birds, a master copywriter who is also a master copywriting teacher.

He has made himself, his partners, his clients, and — most important for you — many of his students and readers wealthy. While he is adept in many areas of business, his greatest strength — the key area that is the foundation for so much of his success — is his mastery of a deceptively simple skill: the ability to write persuasive sales letters.

Sales letters written by Michael Masterson or under his direction have mailed in the millions, and have generated millions of dollars in sales for him and his clients. In this book, *The Architecture of Persuasion*, he teaches you his simple five-step formula for writing sales letters that have beaten countless controls, launched over a dozen multimillion-dollar businesses, and generated sales and profits most direct marketers only dream about.

I said that writing persuasive sales letters is a deceptively simple skill. After all, almost everyone can write a letter. But few people can write sales letters that follow Michael Masterson's time-tested "architecture" of persuasion. Now you will be one of them.

But you won't acquire the skill merely by reading this book. You will acquire it by putting Michael's techniques to work and practicing them, writing letter after letter according to the Masterson formula.

Writing sales letters is like playing the piano. Easy to do poorly; extremely difficult to do well. Most marketers are good at writing mediocre sales letters. Michael Masterson can make you great at writing letters that compel your prospective customers to order your products and send you their checks.

You've surely heard the old saying "Those who can, do; those who can't, teach." It is our good fortune that Michael Masterson does both, and does them better than just about anyone on the planet.

  — Robert W. Bly, author, *The Copywriter's Handbook* (Henry Holt)

Introduction

The Architecture of the Sales Letter

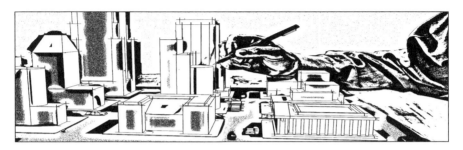

Of all the many forms of direct-response marketing copy none is more fundamental than the simple sales letter.

Sales letters have been around for as long as man has been writing letters. You could argue that the poems of Sappho, written more than two thousand years ago, were letters selling love.

Mark Twain made a part-time living writing sales copy. So did F. Scott Fitzgerald and Ogden Nash. Direct-response sales letters have been around for at least two hundred years — since mail was carried on horseback. The only other direct-response vehicle that can claim such a pedigree is the catalog.

These days, many fledgling copywriters write exclusively for websites and blogs. They may have some familiarity with "older" formats, such as magalogs, bookalogs, and reportalogs, but most have never written an actual sales letter. That's a shame. And a problem.

For nothing will teach you the art and science of good copywriting faster and better than writing sales letters.

On the face of it, writing a sales letter is a simple matter.

- You begin with a "teaser" — copy printed on the outside of the envelope.
- Then you write a headline for the top of the letter.
- Then you write the letter itself, selling the product.
- And finally, you "close" the letter by asking for the sale.

What could be easier than that?

Yet most copywriters coming into the market don't have the skill to do it. And this lack of skill shows through in the abysmal quality of writing that is ubiquitous on the Internet today.

Because of the Internet's rapid growth, thousands and thousands of copywriters have flooded into the market recently. Most of them have no experience or education in the field. Some take the occasional home-study course that covers the basics but offers neither feedback nor the opportunity to practice. Others take lessons from self-dubbed experts who have never competed in (let alone made a name for themselves in) the real world of direct mail — which is dominated by sales letters.

Some of these ersatz copywriters will eke out a living writing ersatz copy for marginal websites and e-zines. A few will break through by hard work and continuous self-education. Most will find copywriting to be a difficult and unrewarding profession and will move on to other careers.

Meanwhile, the opportunity for an intellectually rewarding and financially remunerative career in copywriting has never been greater. The direct-marketing industry is, and always has been, the fastest-growing advertising medium. Its growth rate has never dipped below double digits. By the early 1990s, it was already larger than any other advertising channel — larger than newspaper advertising, larger than magazine advertising, larger even than television or cable advertising. In fact, globally, it was already larger than all other forms of advertising put together!

And that was in the early 1990s. Now consider this: When Bill Clinton was elected in 1992, there were only 53 sites on the World Wide Web. By the time he left office in 2000, there were 9 million. Today, there are more than 200 million websites and thousands of new ones are going online every day!

Because of its interactive capabilities, the Internet is the perfect medium for direct-response marketing. And because of its low barriers to entry, it is equally perfect for entrepreneurship. What this means is that there is a huge and growing need for individuals who can write strong sales copy. But this fast-growing tide of demand will be met by an equally fast-growing wall of consumer resistance. For the Internet is a two-headed beast. On the one side, it offers the copywriter access to a global marketplace of readers. On the other side, it has made it easy for those readers to become sophisticated consumers who can distinguish good advertising from bad and genuine promises from specious fakery.

To be a successful copywriter and enjoy the financial and personal rewards of being at the crest of this tidal wave of growth, you must master the art and science of persuasion. And there is no better or faster way to do that than to learn how to write a good, simple sales letter.

Mastering the sales letter will give you a big advantage over copywriters who don't have this skill. When you are called upon to analyze a marketing campaign or discuss a specific promotion you will know what you are talking about. You will understand every aspect of the creative process — from identifying the purpose of the campaign to researching the prospect and the product and designing a selling strategy that correctly links the two.

You can learn to do that over time, but you'll accelerate the learning process enormously by mastering the direct-mail sales letter.

The Elements of a Classic Sales Letter

The traditional, direct-mail sales letter has the following physical elements:

- **An envelope**

The typical envelope is white, rectangular, unimposing. But there are many other options both in terms of size and finish. All envelopes carry a name, address, and stamp or meter mark. Most include a return address. Whether you put teaser copy on the outside of the envelope — and if so, what copy — are critically important creative decisions. The right choice can double or triple the letter's response rate. The wrong choice can drastically depress it.

You're invited to join a small group of subscribers who could have made **ONE MILLION DOLLARS** on just 1 recommendation a week.

Want to know their secret?
SEE INSIDE...

- **A sales letter**

This is the main element that comes out of the envelope, the piece the reader will usually read first. A typical sales letter carries a headline on top — often the same words that were printed on the outside of the envelope — followed by a salutation, lead, sales argument, and close. It can range from as few as four pages to as many as 40 or 50.

"Each week, I tell my readers to make just 1 investment buy. And last year, not one pick lost value!

Just 2 in 2004, 4 in 2003!

" It's no wonder our readers could have turned $5,000 into $1 MILLION in just over 5 years! Read on to find out how!"
— Steve Sarnoff, Editor, Options Hotline

* *

 Since Steve Sarnoff, options guru, relaunched his exclusive e-mail Alert Service, *Options Hotline*, on Oct. 24, 1999, with an initial $5,000 recommendation to buy Barrick calls...the profit opportunities for his readers have just doubled and tripled and quadrupled... again and again and again.

That $5,000 would have grown to a quarter of a million on Dec. 3, 2000.

Then half a million dollars on Sept. 30, 2002.

And then to...$1 MILLION on Dec. 2, 2004!

His track record: <u>100% winners in 2005</u>!...<u>95% winners in 2004</u>! <u>91% in 2003</u>! Steve's record just keeps getting better and better!

WOW! $1 MILLION in a little over five years with a startup investment of just $5,000! I'm so sorry you missed the ride. But get ready. Because you're invited to:

Join Steve as he shows you the way to $1 MILLION... it's simple and straightforward and we'll show you how with Steve's one weekly option buy recommendation

His readers call him "prophetic." <u>Read on to find out why</u>...

* *

Dear Future Millionaire,

The stock market of the past few years has produced very few millionaires. You just can't make a million dollars with a $5,000 initial investment on a seven-year average annual return of 1.25%. To do so would take you more than 426 years. You'll never live to see it, and neither will your grandchildren, great-grandchildren, even your great-great-grandchildren.

Hello, I'm Steve Sarnoff, recognized options expert and the editor of **Options Hotline**. I'm here to tell you that even if you've never traded options before, you can do it. In fact, it's quite

(over, please)

- **A lift note**

Generally speaking, the lift note is short, printed in a way that looks like it was handwritten or typewritten, and signed by someone other than the person who signed the main letter. It often talks about the product from an entirely different perspective.

Communication Briefings
                                    Douglas J. Manoni, CEO

Dear Friend,

The colleague who never meets a deadline ...

The employee who responds to constructive criticism by pouting for a week ...

The boss who refuses to listen to your ideas ...

WHAT WE HAVE HERE IS A FAILURE TO COMMUNICATE!

But what's the solution?

For more than 50,000 loyal subscribers, the solution is an eight-page monthly newsletter called COMMUNICATION BRIEFINGS.

Our readers typically spend just 15 minutes with each issue. In return, they receive a wealth of wisdom on how to use communication to solve their problems at work.

Management problems. Discipline problems. "People" problems. Even the kind of grammaar and spelling problems you face when you sit down to write a memo or report.

My problem today is a tough one. How can I get you to subscribe to a newsletter you've never seen?

My solution is simply to let you see it without risk or obligation. Read as many issues as you want -- even all 12, if necessary -- before you make your final decision.

Then if COMMUNICATION BRIEFINGS is not for you, let me know and I'll send all your money back. Every penny of it. You can keep all the issues you've received and keep all the free bonus gifts we've sent you too.

So if you're suffering from a "failure to communicate" at work, I've got the solution. Start your trial subscription to COMMUNICATION BRIEFINGS today!

Sincerely,

Douglas J. Manoni

Douglas J. Manoni, CEO

- **A brochure or flyer**

Many direct-mail sales packages include a little booklet that explains the benefits of certain product features. Very often, it is printed on coated paper and produced with four-color processing. To be effective, brochures or flyers must have a good reason for being. They must stand on their own, yet support the ideas presented in the sales letter.

Time-tested Million-Dollar Secrets a Father Only Reveals to His Son...

My dad Paul Sarnoff was one of the legends in options trading for more than 40 years. Wall Street turned to my dad for the best in options trading advice. He is to options what Warren Buffett is to stocks — a genius! In fact, it was my dad who started **Options Hotline**, his private options advisory service available only to a select few, back in 1989.

About 30 years ago, my dad brought me into the "family business" — sort of a Sarnoff & Son. For years, I literally soaked up every word he ever spoke about trading options for big profits. I watched him trade. I listened carefully to his reasons. I analyzed his every pick. I did what he did. It was awesome to watch a master at work.

As his apprentice, I saw firsthand how my dad raked in profits. And I'll always remember what my dad said to me nearly every day: "Son, options are the best...perhaps the only way to get rich very quickly."

While I was learning trading secrets from my dad, I also earned my college degree, worked on the floor of the Commodity Exchange and founded my own research company, developing my own charting and analytical techniques to build on what my father had taught me.

In 1995, Dad asked me to join him as co-editor of **Options Hotline**. I was proud that this options genius felt I was ready to join him as his equal. Sadly, my dad passed away in 1999, but his legacy lives on through me and the ongoing success of **Options Hotline**.

My first solo recommendation was Barrick Gold calls on Oct. 24, 1999. Not my best pick, with a 100% loss, but I made up for it with my next four picks...

- Home Depot calls — 289%
- AMEX calls — 150%
- Disney calls — 315%
- Cisco calls — 386%

In fact, my next nine recommendations were all double — and triple-digit winners!

As a subscriber to **Options Hotline**, you'll get more than 50 years of my dad's options experience...combined with my 30 years of technical analysis...for 80 years of options experience you can depend on to give you the winning picks.

I just don't know where you would find a more authoritative source for profiting from options. But don't take my word for it. Read what Dr. Robinson, a longtime subscriber, said... *"I have followed your father's recommendations and now yours. I am very pleased. I am very impressed by your ability to pick specific trades with prophetic wisdom. Somehow you know what's going to happen before the rest of us do!"*

Now, you can get the powerful money-making secrets only found in *Options Hotline*. Order online right now at www.agorafinancial.com/orderonline.html, call toll free at 1-800-682-0865, or return the enclosed no-risk order form in the postage paid envelope provided.

- **A buckslip**

This is a piece of paper, generally the size and shape of a dollar bill, that gives the reader an additional reason to buy or offers the reader an additional assurance that buying would be a rational choice.

- **An order device**

The order device can sometimes be part of the sales letter, but more often it is a standalone card that restates the main sales idea, spells out the offer, and guarantees satisfaction.

Each of these elements serves a different purpose. To write an effective sales letter, the copywriter must know what those different purposes are. More important, he must develop the specific skills necessary to achieve those purposes. And, finally, he must understand the fundamental psychology of the selling process itself. If he can do that, he will never be confused or misled by the wrong-headed and shallow "rules" of copywriting that are so abundantly supplied by self-proclaimed copywriting geniuses whose only success in direct marketing has come from passing themselves off as experts.

To illustrate what I mean by wrong-headed and shallow ideas, let's analyze one of the most popular: the concept that "the one and only purpose of the envelope is to get itself opened."

If that were the only — or most important — purpose of the envelope copy, why wouldn't the following teaser always work best?

Inside: Free Money!

Or:

Inside: Carefree Sex!

Or:

Inside: Eternal Happiness!

There is a good reason such extreme teasers are rarely used. They don't work. And why don't they work? It's not that they won't get the envelope opened. They probably would. It's that they will disappoint the reader once he discovers that there is, indeed, no free money or sex or happiness waiting for him on the inside.

If the main purpose of envelope copy really is to *get the envelope opened*, such deceptive teasers would be the rule rather than the exception. An official-looking envelope with "Check Enclosed" or one that appears to be from the IRS will almost always get itself opened. But how will the reader feel when he examines the contents and discovers he's been tricked?

Some copywriting experts recommend "blank" envelopes — envelopes on which teaser copy is omitted, the address is impact-printed, and a live stamp is used — because they are almost always opened. Studies confirm this. But envelopes that are opened with greater frequency do not necessarily *sell* better. In the 30 years I've been looking at direct-marketing packages, I've seen hundreds of blank-versus-teaser tests. In many cases, blank envelopes *did* work better. But in many cases, they did not. And I can think of only a very few blockbuster breakthrough promotions that used a blank envelope.

If you want to compete in today's booming global direct-response market, you have to write envelope teasers that do more than merely get the prospect to open the envelope.

You have to be able to get your readers to open your sales letter with exactly the right thoughts and feelings of expectation. You have to do *more* than manipulate their emotions. You must engage them in a deep and permanent way. And you can't do that unless you really understand the psychology of persuasion.

I spent the first 10 years of my marketing career writing sales letters. I spent the following 20 years coaching copywriters. Over that time, I became familiar with all the main direct-mail formats: catalogs, bookalogs, space ads, newsletters, etc. Each of these, I discovered, had its own particular characteristics. But beneath them all, there were certain universal principles.

Because the sales letter is the simplest form of direct-response advertising, I found it to be the best vehicle for teaching these universal principles. If you came to me to learn copywriting — even today in the age of the Internet — I'd start off by teaching you what I'm going to cover in this book.

In the several hours it will take you to read this book, you will get an understanding of my most important secrets.

- You will learn, for example, that every effective sale is made at two levels: an initial appeal that is based on deeply seated emotional factors and a secondary appeal that is based on logic and consistency.

- You will be able to write envelope teasers that do much more than just get the envelope opened.

- You will discover why the beginning of the sales letter is the most important part — in most cases, accounting for 80 percent of the letter's power.

- You will know exactly how to "seal" the deal after you have caught the prospect's interest.

- You will know when to close the letter "falsely" and when to do it *for real*.

- You will know exactly how each of the five basic elements of a sales letter work so that you will never be wondering, "What do I write now?"

- You will discover the purpose, problem, and possibility of each of the five elements — which will make you a stronger, faster, and more effective copywriter than 95 percent of the writers with whom you are competing.

In Chapter One, I'll reveal to you the main purpose, problem, and possibility of each of the five elements: (1) the envelope teaser, (2) the sales letter headline, (3) the lead, (4) the sales argument, and (5) the close. Then, beginning with Chapter Two, we will look closely at how these elements work. We will do that by using an extended metaphor: the sales letter as a romantic encounter with a beautiful woman.

This is going to be an easy read. And a fun read too. But we are going to cover a lot of ground. So be prepared to read this book again and again. By the time you master the principles I'm about to explain, you should be able to outline your sales promotions confidently, write your leads quickly, and write copy that has fewer mistakes and a higher likelihood of success.

In a relatively short period of time (perhaps half the time it would take otherwise), you'll be writing at a completely higher level and earning (let's not forget earning) a lot more money.

You'll be able to recognize, almost instantly, fatal weaknesses in copy (either in your own first drafts or in other people's work) and correct them. Just as important, you will have a way to talk about copy in pragmatic terms, with a vocabulary that is both functional and expressive.

In short, this little book will make you a smarter, quicker, stronger, and more confident copywriter — which, in turn, will make you happier, healthier, and wiser. And it all begins right now!

Are you ready for a personal transformation of a very practical kind?

Let's go then ...

1

The Copywriter's Challenge

The only thing writers like better than metaphors are extended metaphors. So, as a writer, you'll appreciate what awaits you here — a detailed comparison between writing a successful sales letter and initiating a romantic relationship.

Many marketing experts like to compare business to war. Some best-selling books have taken good advantage of this obvious metaphor. In *Sun Tzu Was a Sissy*, for example, Stanley Bing says:

"In the business war...one must be prepared for a low level of conflict sustained over a period of time, perhaps indefinitely. On occasion, that nagging, aggravating buzz of battle kicks up to lethal proportions, then sinks down again into a dangerous but nontoxic 'business as usual' zone. The war goes on and on and on. And there is nothing you can do to stop it except fight in it until either you or it is done."

I don't like the martial metaphor, because it views the customer as an enemy — someone to be tricked or bullied into submission. As a short-term strategy, this can sometimes work.

And the direct-response universe abounds in promotional copy that badgers, beats, or bullshits the prospect into making a purchase. Smart copywriters eschew this approach, because they know that it is ultimately destructive and self-defeating.

Business should not be like war. It should be like love. And not a steamy, one night stand, but a mutually beneficial, steadily improving romance that lasts a lifetime.

Love and War in the Market

The psychological value of loving your customers is easy to understand. If the copy you write benefits those who read it, you will feel better about the time you spend writing it. The material value of loving your customers is less easy to prove. That's because marketing that browbeats or bamboozles is often effective — at least in the beginning.

The direct-marketing industry is huge (estimated at $2 trillion in 2008, according to the Direct Marketing Association) and extremely competitive. In such a big, bustling arena, it's tough for a new copywriter to break in. Often it feels like battlefield tactics are needed to succeed. When you look at the success some companies have hyping inferior products to unsuspecting prospects, it may seem futile to take a more caring approach.

But for every marketing campaign that involves trickiness or emotional manipulation, there is an equally strong but more elegant one that works through enthusiasm, honesty, and goodwill.

The advantages of loving, rather than conquering, your customers have never been greater than they are today. That's because of the Internet. Your customers and potential customers have access to all kinds of information about the company you work for and the products you are selling. If you finagle people out of their dollars, they will share their bad buying experiences with everyone searching the Web. It won't take long for those products to develop a bad Internet reputation. And that will make it much harder for you to write successful promotions to sell them in the future.

The single most important way for a copywriter to love his customers is to write sincere, truthful copy that promotes a good product — a product that solves a customer's problem or helps her achieve a goal. Good products make copywriting easier, because there is more substance to them. They have advantages that inferior products lack. Good products usually have strong benefits that a copywriter can convert to verbal gold. When you write copy for good products being sold by good companies, you are in a very favorable financial position — where the commercial relationship is always getting better and more valuable for everyone involved, including the company, the customer ... and you.

So the copywriter's challenge is a laudable one: to improve the world one sale at a time by promoting products that solve problems and/or help people achieve goals. If you take that challenge seriously, you will commit to working for clients whose products you admire and selling those products with integrity. This book provides an outline for doing that with a simple sales letter:

- how to identify the most important truths about the product and present them with the greatest appeal

- how to deal with any perceived shortcomings directly and positively

- how to write copy that is always gripping and moves customers emotionally while answering their rational questions

As a beginning copywriter, it might feel as though you don't have the power to determine what kind of copy you will write (copy that loves versus copy that conquers), let alone what kind of products you will sell (good versus not-so-good). In fact, you have complete control.

There are many techniques in the copywriting trade. Most of them are useful and honest. But some of them are not. As you develop your skills, keep asking yourself ... "Will this help me love the customer? Or will this help me fool her?" Reject the weapons of war. And reject the martial artists who sell them to you. Begin your career as a copywriting lover, not a fighter, and you will always be doubly blessed — with good money and goodwill.

Okay. Now that you have heard my little speech about love and war, let's go back to one of the ideas I presented in the Introduction to this book — that every complete sales letter has five elements, and each element has a purpose, a problem, and a possibility.

The Five Essential Elements of a Sales Letter

These five elements form two parts that are sometimes called the "front" and the "back" of the sales letter.

The front:

1. The envelope teaser

2. The sales letter teaser (headline)

3. The lead

The back:

4. The body (or sales argument)

5. The close

The front of a sales letter has a different purpose than the back. That's because, in writing the first part of the sales letter, the copywriter faces different problems than he faces in the second half.

Let's talk about these problems for a moment — the practical problems posed by each of the five elements.

The problem the envelope copy poses is this:

The average direct-mail reader receives between six and nine sales letters a day, yet opens only one or two. What words can you write on the envelope to keep her from tossing your sales letter in the trash?

A slightly different problem presents itself a moment later, after your prospect has opened the envelope and opened the letter. What words can you put above the salutation that will ensure she keeps reading?

If your prospect does continue to read, she is going to read with a certain amount of skepticism. She may be very interested in what you have said so far (on the envelope and at the top of the letter), but she has read many sales letters before, some of which have disappointed her. So she is reading with a high level of expectation. The copywriter's problem is that unless he is very persuasive very quickly, the prospect will think, "Oh, I know what this is. Another sales letter. I've seen this kind of thing before." And if she thinks that, she will stop reading and not complete the sale.

Those are the three problems you face in the front part of the letter. If you overcome them, then you run into two more problems that you must solve in the back part. Both of these problems involve the prospect's rational mind. And both can be solved rationally.

In brief, the five problems are:

1. Envelope teaser: "This is junk mail. It's not for me."

2. Headline: "Damn! I've been fooled again."

3. Lead: "I know what this is. I'm not interested."

4. Sales argument: "This is no different than other, similar products I've bought before."

5. Close: "It's a good product, but should I buy it at this time?"

Beyond Purpose and Problem to Possibility

As a copywriter who wants to be competitive in today's exploding direct-marketing industry, you should understand the *purpose* and *problem* of each of the five elements of a sales letter.

If you want to elevate your copywriting power to the highest level, though, you should also understand how to ratchet up the copy for each element — to make it catchier and more compelling than the rest of what is out there in the marketplace. To achieve this higher level, you must understand what can be done — what higher purpose or possibility can be achieved with every element of the sales letter.

With the envelope teaser, for example, an A-level copywriter is not content with getting the prospect to open the envelope. He wants to accomplish something more. What he hopes to do is get the prospect to open the envelope in *a frame of mind that is conducive to reading the sales letter with positive anticipation*.

The higher purpose or possibility of the headline is to intensify that positive anticipation.

And the higher purpose or possibility of the lead is to broaden and deepen that anticipation into a subtle bundle of thoughts and feelings that leave the prospect thinking, *"This is really good! I'm very glad I'm reading this letter!"*

Beyond eradicating any fears, doubts, or skepticism the prospect might have about the offer, the sales argument offers the A-level copywriter the chance to thoroughly and irreversibly show her that buying the product is *the rational thing to do*. And a deftly executed close will leave the prospect delighted with her rational decision to buy — proud of herself for having encountered some extra, unexpected benefit for making such a smart move.

In summary then, here are the five possibilities:

- The higher purpose of the teaser is to get the prospect to open the envelope with the right expectations.

- The higher purpose of the headline is to get her to read the lead with the right emotional feeling.

- The higher purpose of the lead is to get the prospect excited about reading the rest of the letter and emotionally open to the sale.

- The higher purpose of the sales argument is to get the prospect to rationalize the emotional conclusion she has already arrived at: that buying the product will help her.

- And the higher purpose of the close is to get rid of any residual skepticism and replace it with a positive and expectant feeling about the commercial relationship between customer and company.

In the following chapters — by using an extended metaphor comparing the structure of a successful sales letter to the initiation of a romantic relationship — I will examine each of those purposes, problems, and possibilities and show you how you can use your knowledge of them to create powerful, impeccable, and highly successful direct-response sales promotions.

Here's how our story begins ...

The Romantic Challenge

Imagine this:

You are a college professor. A professor of archeology at a small, liberal arts college in New England. You have lived an exciting life. You have traveled the world, discovering rare artifacts and experiencing exciting adventures. You have written books about your findings and have won many awards. There is only one thing missing: someone to share it all with.

You have a maiden aunt who wants to see you happily married. She has been encouraging you to start dating for years, but your career obligations and natural shyness have interfered.

Now, on her death bed, she has given you a dramatic ulti-matum: Find a suitable romantic partner before the end of the day and inherent her vast fortune ... or fail to do so and receive nothing.

Here's what you have to do:

- Go into town and find someone with whom you'd like to have a long-term, romantic relationship.

- Convince her to come back home with you.

- Get her inside your house, and make her fall in love with you.

- Persuade her to come upstairs to your bedroom and begin the relationship you both now desire by surrendering her precious self to you.

- Do all of this before midnight.

That is — I'm sure you'd agree — a considerable challenge. You have to pick someone who doesn't know you or anything about you. And you have to consummate a relationship — with-out lies or force — within a single night. To accomplish such a task, you are going to have to be very persuasive. It's highly un-likely that you will succeed unless you do everything right.

But that is what you have to do every time you sit down to write a sales letter. Every sales letter has the same objective: to convince someone you don't know (and who doesn't know you) to do something she's skeptical about doing — giving away her money to buy a product she has never heard about before.

And because you are in the service of a good company (a company that wants to develop long-term relationships with its customers), you have to further convince this prospect that she is buying into a beneficial commercial relationship — one that will include the purchase of many more products in the future.

Are you with me?

So imagine yourself more clearly now. You are an archeology professor, an archeology professor who specializes in retrieving ancient artifacts. In fact, you are a sort of Indiana Jones. Brilliant. Adventuresome. Good looking. Altogether, you are a very attractive guy — especially to the sort of woman who has always fantasized about Indiana Jones.

You have less than 24 hours to find your romantic counterpart. There's no time to lose.

Brothels, Bars, and Brownstones — Where Should You Start Looking?

The easiest place to find a willing gal would be the local brothel. But it's highly unlikely that your aunt would approve of the type of person you'd find there. This is about finding a long-term lover, you remind yourself. The brothel is out.

What about a local bar? There are two that come to mind. One is a noisy honky-tonk by the harbor. The other is a wood-paneled pub that caters to stock brokers. The honky-tonk is likely to be filled with party girls who would not appreciate your intelligence. And the pub will be populated by ladies who wouldn't appreciate your roguish charm.

You are looking for a suitable match — someone who will be awed by your worldliness and captivated by your academic accomplishments. Where would you find someone like that?

Well, it just so happens that you are in luck. There is a party being held tonight for the National Explorers Society at a beautiful, 19th century brownstone in the historic district. Hundreds of people will be there, including dozens of attractive women who have a weakness for archeology and Indiana Jones-type guys.

You are happy to know about the Explorers Society event, because you know it will provide you with the chance to meet lots of potential lovers — and you know you may have to make several (if not many) attempts at wooing them before you can find one willing to come back to your home.

In the world of direct-response marketing, when you go to this party it's like what happens when your sales letter is sent to an intelligently assembled mailing list of qualified potential customers.

Getting to Know Your Prospect

One of the great things about direct-response marketing is how much available information there is about the people you are selling to. This gives you a big advantage as a copywriter, because it allows you to get an impression of the kind of consumers your prospects are.

The task of selecting the names to mail to is the job of the company's marketing manager, the person who manages the production and mailing of the sales letter for your client.

As a copywriter, you have the right to ask the marketing manager about the mailing lists he is compiling. And smart copywriters do that. They find out which lists are going to be used and study the characteristics (demographics and buying patterns) of the names on those lists to get a good idea of the way their prospects think and behave when it comes to buying the kind of product they are going to try to sell to them.

The easiest way to get this information is to ask the marketing manager for the data card for each mailing list he will be using for your sales letter.

The data cards are provided by the list broker. And you'll find two kinds of information on them. First, you'll find a good deal that you don't need — mailing restrictions, list maintenance, list pricing. That's because the chief function of the data card is to rent out the mailing list. It's not designed to help the copywriter.

But you will also find lots of information that you do need. This includes demographic data (such as your prospects' age, sex, and sometimes political affiliations), a brief profile of their personal characteristics and interests, and list "usage" information — which tells you the names of other companies that are using that particular list and what products they are selling.

This is very valuable stuff. The list usage info is especially interesting, because it gives you a way to find out the most important thing about the person to whom you will be writing: her buying habits and preferences.

It also gives you a way to find out the names of companies that have been renting that same list *repeatedly* so you can get your hands on the promotions they've been mailing. If they've rented the same list multiple times, it tells you their mailings to those names have been working well.

Study those promotions, as well as all the previous promotions your client has mailed in the past year or two for the product you'll be selling. Study the strong ones to discover themes and promises that might have "worked." Study the weak ones to identify themes and promises that didn't.

Don't plagiarize from the strong packages, but do try to take advantage of any insights you get from them.

Talk to your client's marketing manager, too. Get his take on who the company's customers are and why they buy the products they buy. If possible, speak to current customers to find out why they think they bought the product you'll be selling, what they liked about it and what they didn't.

This will give you a very good idea about how to approach your prospect. About what subjects to bring up in your sales copy and even what kind of language to use.

Most copywriters won't go to the trouble of reading demographics on data cards, let alone collecting and studying high-usage promotions and talking to actual customers. So just think what an advantage doing all this will give you when you sit down to write a promotion. It's practically like having a blue-print that tells you where the money is hidden!

Ignoring this valuable data is a big mistake. Don't do it.

So that brings us back to our romantic challenge: to go to the Explorers Society party and talk one of the eligible bachelor-ettes there to come back to your home and physically initiate a long-term relationship with you. The head of your department at the college has given you a free ticket to get inside. You spend the afternoon thinking about how wonderful it will be if you are able to find and seduce the right gal. In one night, you will have accomplished two goals: finding a soul mate and achieving life-long financial security.

Wouldn't it be nice?!

2

Opening Lines: The Envelope Teaser

The Three P's of the Envelope Teaser

- **Purpose:** to get the prospect to open the envelope with the right expectations

- **Problem:** to convince the prospect, in just a few seconds, not to throw it in the trash

- **Possibility:** to get the prospect to open the envelope with a frame of mind that is conducive to reading the sales letter with positive anticipation

---

It is 6:30. You are standing in your bedroom in your underwear, deciding what to wear. There is a book on the dressing table called *Dressing for Success*. It is opened to a chapter on Formal Events.

The book advises that "the clothes you select should reflect two things: the event and the person you are."

The event has been described as semi-formal, so, in theory, a suit jacket would do. You have one suit — a conservative, three-piece pinstripe from Savile Row — and an old tuxedo. The tuxedo would be acceptable, but would not reflect who you are. You are, after all, an Indiana Jones-type archeology professor looking for a lady who will appreciate someone like you. The three-piece suit would make the wrong statement, just as surfing shorts and flip-flops would.

To present the full effect of your swashbuckling self, you select a brown suede jacket, beige chinos, and a fine pair of ankle-high hiking boots. You finish off the outfit with a sturdy, leather-banded sports watch, a copper wristband, and a silver talisman peeking from the open collar of your white linen shirt.

You stand back and examine your reflection in the mirror. Looking back at you is a striking figure. A handsome yet rugged gentleman who will attract attention without looking garish or inappropriate. Yes, the look is good. But then you have an inspiration. You unbutton one of your shirt collar tabs and push up the collar a little. This gives your outfit the slightest bit of extra edginess, for something is awry. It sends a subtle message that your intuition tells you might work in your favor: that this Indiana Jones could use a little TLC.

Now, you are ready!

How does this relate to the sales letter?

Dressing the Envelope

In direct-response marketing, the sales message is of the utmost importance. But the appearance of the envelope and its contents matters too. What you should aim for is to make the package not only attractive to your prospect but also appropriate for both the product and the sentiments expressed by the copy. Speaking specifically of the envelope, you want to make sure that its size, shape, color, and quality look appealing and mesh well with the product you are selling and the teaser you will be putting on the outside.

As a copywriter, you may get some help here. Some of the marketers you work with may be very savvy about the physical elements of a direct-response mailing. They may understand that the envelope should match the tone of the sales message. In taking on a copywriting assignment, don't be shy about asking for input on the selection of the envelope — and don't be reluctant to express your own opinion either. You may not get final say, but you should do everything you can to make sure your copy is supported rather than undermined by the look of the package.

If the product you're selling is upscale and exclusive, then the envelope should look upscale and exclusive. That might be best expressed by a white or cream-colored envelope made from high-quality stock. If the product is a discounted offer, the envelope should look the part — made from inexpensive paper in a color that screams "cheap."

You may notice that while most marketers select fine stationery for upscale offers, few are smart enough to select cheap-looking stock for down-market promotions. There is a common illusion in the direct-response industry that it's good to put discounted offers in fancy envelopes. The idea is that it increases the perceived value of the offer. In fact, that is almost always a big mistake.

If you are at the lower end of the market, be happy to project yourself as a source of low-end goods. You don't want your prospects looking at envelopes that suggest high end, because they will feel intimidated (even if at a subconscious level). In designing the envelope, your objective should be to make your prospects feel at home. If they eat McDonald's, make the envelope feel like McDonald's, not like Ruth's Chris Steak House.

When you are involved in this important but often neglected creative process, remember the advice of our archeology professor's style book: Select something that is both attractive and appropriate.

Conjuring Up Your Opening Line

It is now 7:30. You are at the party, standing at the bar, sipping a glass of chilled Padron tequila. The band is playing jazz. There are all sorts of ladies milling about. Many of them are attractive. You feel good about your chances of finding someone suitable here. Thank goodness you came here instead of a pub, you think. This is the right place.

You feel good, but you are not exactly sure what to do. You are not accustomed to "picking up" women (let alone romancing them so quickly). But you can't just stand there hoping one will come up to you.

You have to take action. What you need is an *opening line.* Something you can say that will attract attention without causing discomfort or embarrassment. Something that will make your chosen lady want to continue talking to you so you can eventually invite her to your home.

You spot a woman who looks perfect. She is good looking, well-dressed, but not stuffy. Judging by her interaction with those around her, she seems to have a good sense of humor. She is chatting with an older woman at the other end of the bar. She is holding a book in one hand, and sipping what appears to be a Singapore Sling in the other.

You have an instinct that she is the right one. But what should you do? Should you walk over boldly or timidly? Should you sit down on the stool beside her, or just stand there politely and wait for her to notice you?

These are similar to the questions the copywriter must ask himself when he contemplates writing the teaser — the sentence or phrase he will use on the outside of the envelope to grab his prospect's attention and make her want to open it and see what's inside.

The outside of the envelope is the first thing the prospect sees when, sorting through her mail, she comes to your promotion. What you put on that envelope — the words you choose and the way they look on the paper — is extremely important. If the message is wrong-headed or printed in such a way that it conveys the wrong emotion, it's highly likely that your prospect will trash your letter without a second thought.

At the Explorers Society party, this would be like saying your opening line to a lady and having her laugh at you and walk away. You don't want that to happen.

What Is Junk Mail, Really?

Junk mail is marketing copy that is false and/ or recognized as false and is thus rejected by the recipient. Sales letters that speak to the heart of the prospect are valued — and are thus carefully read and considered.

There are basically two ways to treat the outer envelope.

1. The simplest way is to make the envelope look as much like first-class mail as possible. First-class mail gets opened at a higher rate than its third-class cousins. Creating an ersatz first-class look, many copywriting gurus argue, will result in the highest "open rate." To do this, use a first-class stamp (or a third-class stamp that looks like a first-class stamp), address the envelope with a laser jet printer instead of a label, and print the bar code away from the address.

2. The second way is to make it obvious that there's a sales letter inside by putting teaser copy on the envelope. (Remember, the purpose of teaser copy is to hook the reader's interest and provoke her to open the envelope.)

As I said in the introduction to this book, some direct-mail experts argue that a blank envelope is always better than an envelope with teaser copy on it. Others argue that teasers are necessary. I have looked at the results of thousands of envelope tests over the years. I can't say that blank envelopes are better than envelopes with teasers or vice versa. What I can say is:

- Blank envelopes do better than bad teasers.

- But good teasers sometimes do better than blank envelopes.

What are good teasers? Those that can get better response rates than blank envelopes.

That bit of logic doesn't help very much, I admit. But maybe this will. Using a first-class approach will get your envelope opened most of the time, so it is always a good idea to use the blank envelope as a default option. But test a teaser too. Persuade the marketing manager to test two envelopes if he can, one blank and one with a teaser. If he agrees, then you will see if the teaser you wrote was strong enough to out-pull the blank envelope. If he doesn't agree and you must choose only one approach, then use a teaser only when you feel confident that it is very good.

The choice between using a blank envelope versus teaser copy is the metaphorical equivalent of choosing between (1) approaching the lady at the end of the bar and just standing there with a smile, hoping she will start a conversation or (2) starting the conversation yourself with a *good opening line.*

A smile from an attractive person is not a bad opening. Much better, certainly, than saying something stupid or clichéd. But if you could say just the right thing — something to make your potential love mate smile, perhaps — that would be better, wouldn't it?

The Two Most Important Characteristics of Effective Persuasion

Remember, you are an intelligent, well-traveled archeologist. You don't want to go up to this attractive, well-educated woman and say something like, "Hey cutie! Wanna go back to my place?"

Being so direct will attract the attention you want, but it will also make you look rude and insensitive. This woman — if she is the right woman for you — would not respond to such crudeness. She needs to be charmed and impressed. Giving her an ordinary pick-up line will disappoint her.

That is one reason you must think hard about your opening words. The other reason relates to your purpose. Your challenge, as you know, is to find a long-term partner ... not a one-night stand. That means finding someone you can love, someone you can admire.

Taking all this into consideration, you realize that what you say to this lady must achieve several objectives. It must:

- attract her attention

- charm or impress her

- represent you truthfully

- be fundamentally sincere

These last two objectives — truth and sincerity — are the *two most important qualities of great copywriting.*

Yes, you must come up with an opening line that is smart, meaningful, and charming. But it must also be true and sincere. Those first few words will be the first words this marvelous woman hears you say. They will make an impression that will be enduring. They will determine how she reacts to you immediately and how she sees you for the rest of your life together.

> Master Copywriter's Tip: If you have the choice, suggest a "split test" to your client. Test half the file with a blank envelope and the other half with teaser copy. Writing a teaser that must compete against (what appears to be) personal correspondence is a challenge. That's good, because you need to be challenged to write really good envelope copy.

As a copywriter, you have a big responsibility. You must write copy that has the potential to create a good, long-term relationship between your client and your prospect. That means choosing words that will start the relationship right. That's why it's important to take the time to write dozens of teasers and select the very best one. It has to be a teaser that makes the prospect think, if only for a second, "This envelope might contain something very special. Something I've been seeking for a long time!"

You can't provoke that thought with a clichéd teaser. Only the right phrase will do. It must be something that communicates the value not only of the product but of the relationship you are seeking to start.

This brings us to our first application of the Three P's: purpose, problem, and possibility.

The Purpose of the Envelope Teaser

Just as the purpose of your opening line at the Explorers Society is to start a conversation with the woman at the bar, the purpose of the envelope teaser is to get the prospect to open the envelope.

The Problem of the Envelope Teaser

One way to get the prospect to open the envelope would be to say something outlandish or bribe her in some way. You could, for example, achieve a 100 percent open rate simply by printing "Cash Inside! Open Immediately!" on the front.

But you couldn't possibly deliver on that promise, and so would be setting up your client for a very bad relationship down the line.

You could try something honest and straightforward, such as "Great Product Inside at 50% Off." But that kind of teaser creates a different sort of problem. The sales pitch is so obvious that you risk having the promotion trashed on the spot.

Outlandish and direct teasers create a good deal of psychological resistance. The bigger or more aggressive the promise, the greater the resistance.

The End of Postal Mail?

According to the USPS, the average household receives 28 pieces of mail per week. That number has actually increased in recent years, despite the proliferation of Internet e-mail.

(Source: *Postal Facts 2007*, USPS)

The Possibility of a Good Envelope Teaser

A good teaser will get the envelope opened. But it will also do something else. It will provoke a receptive attitude, not resistance. If you can arouse a receptive attitude in your prospect, you will have a much easier time with your sales letter. Your prospect will be willing to read a little further into the letter. She will be more open to the claims and promises you will soon be making. She will subconsciously *want* to be sold. That is what a great teaser will do — not just get the prospect to open the envelope but to open it with a predisposition to buy!

Teasers: Bad ... Better ... Best

In *The Copywriter's Handbook*, an excellent guide to direct-mail advertising copy, master copywriter Bob Bly says this about teaser copy:

> *Teasers are effective only when the message is compelling. For example, I'd have a hard time ignoring an envelope with the teaser, "Inside: The Secret to Living Longer and Feeling Better ...Without Dieting or Special Exercise." On the other hand, you'd probably save yourself the trouble of opening an envelope that began, "Sawyer Life Insurance Announces 50th Year of Operation ... Quality Service to the Community for Over Half a Century."*

Bob goes on to suggest that most teasers fall into one of three basic categories …

Category 1: This Is the Best Widget Ever Made

Category 2: This Widget May Save You Up to $500

Category 3: Enclosed Is Your Free Widget

The Category 1 teaser is the weakest, Bob points out, because it is "pure boasting." It is about the product and ignores the reader. "The reader's reaction to the smug claim," Bob says, "will be to throw the mailing away."

It would be like walking up to that beautiful woman at the Explorers Society party and saying, "I am the most interesting and loveable person you have ever met." Imagine how she would react to that!

Take a look at the following:

Can you see why this teaser falls into Category 1? It makes a bold claim: *Practical Sailor* is more "daring" than other sailing magazines. This claim is not entirely self-serving, however. There is an implied benefit to the reader.

What would you say that implied benefit is?

In my mind it is some "brazen" information the magazine will feature that will improve the reader's sailing experience. This implied *promise of benefit* is supported by the offer as explained in the second part of the teaser: The first two issues are free.

Still, this teaser is basically a boast. And for me, it is a boast that doesn't work. Why would a sailor want "daring" or "brazen" information about sailing? Wouldn't he prefer to get ideas and information that is more useful? Information he can use to improve his sailing?

In fact, the name of the magazine — *Practical Sailor* — suggests that pragmatic advice is its unique selling proposition. Thus, the teaser is both boastful and inappropriate. Not a terrible effort, perhaps, but far from a good one.

Let's call this the "narcissistic" teaser from now on, because, like the mythological Narcissus, it is primarily interested in itself.

Now let's look at what Bob Bly calls a Category 2 teaser ("This Widget May Save You Up to $500"). Here is an example:

 **FARMERS**

Gets you back where you belong.*

The "Middleman" could save you $548 a year on your auto insurance.

"My agent is amazing and covered all the bases with me."

"My local agent is outstanding."

"We LOVE our agent ... and his staff. They are beyond helpful and give us the best customer service."

The teaser on the above envelope from Farmers Insurance Group makes a very specific claim: The reader might be eligible for a savings of $548 on her auto insurance. If true, this is a direct and tangible benefit. Anyone paying for auto insurance would likely be interested to find out if she could achieve that level of saving.

Bob Bly says that this type of teaser is stronger than the narcissistic teaser because it gets the reader thinking about a potential future benefit to herself. It is always a good idea to get the prospect thinking about how she can benefit from the intended relationship, Bob says. And he is right.

Let's call this the "potential benefit" teaser. Can you see how much more effective it can be than the narcissistic teaser?

Finally, let's look at Bob's Category 3 type of teaser ("Enclosed Is Your Free Widget"). Here is an example:

Do you see how this kind of teaser might have a stronger emotional impact than either of the other two? Do you see how compelling it could be? That is because it is promising a direct and immediate benefit, not a potential benefit in the future.

Let's call this the "definite benefit" teaser. So now we have identified (with Bob Bly's help) three types of teasers: the narcissistic teaser, the potential benefit teaser, and the definite benefit teaser. We have seen how they work and why potential and definite benefit teasers are usually stronger than narcissistic teasers.

To create definite benefit teasers, Bob suggests nine approaches:

1. **Ask a Question.** ("How Would You Like to Reduce Your Car Insurance Rates by 50%?")

2. **Promise a Benefit.** ("Lose 10 Pounds of Fat in 5 Days With E-Z Diet")

3. **Flatter the Prospect.** ("For You: A Discriminating Art Buyer")

4. **Pique the Reader's Curiosity.** ("Intelligent. Useful. Easy. And Only 5 Cents a Minute.")

5. **Offer a Gift.** ("Free Widget Enclosed")

6. **Extend an Invitation.** ("Your VIP Investor's Invitation Enclosed")

7. **Quote an Authority.** ("FDA Praises New Anti-Cancer Miracle Pill")

8. **Give News.** ("Fed Announces Rate Cut. 10 Stocks That Will Soar.")

9. **Make a Prediction.** ("Oil to Boom Next Year. Here's How to Profit.")

A variation of the definite benefit teaser was developed many years ago by Gene Schwartz, a great copywriter who specialized in selling information products. To entice readers inside the envelope, Schwartz listed a series of "fascinations" — tidbits about interesting information that was revealed within the sales letter itself. Thus the benefits — getting that information — were direct and immediate.

Amazing New Discoveries from Medical Expert Dr. John Heinerman:

1,837 All-Natural PRESCRIPTIONS
For BREAKTHROUGH HEALING!

Bulk Rate
U.S. POSTAGE
PAID
Permit No. 2423
Hartford,CT

My Flu Symptoms Vanished Overnight!
"After drinking this herbal tea I went to bed – by the next morning I was fully recovered"
Healing Prescription on page 88

Lower Blood Pressure!
This herbal compound eases hypertension *and* strengthens the heart.
Healing Prescription on page 226

Super Easy Weight Loss
Breakthrough plant compound burns fat even while you sleep!
Healing Prescription on page 164

I have my Energy Back!
"I feel like a 20-year-old after using this amazing herb – *Thank you* Dr. Heinerman!"
Healing Prescription on page 39

PLUS, TWO FREE GIFTS INSIDE

Try These 100% Drug-Free Prescriptions FREE for 28 days!

Being able to write good definite benefit teasers is a must for anyone hoping to become an A-level copywriter. Definite benefits teasers are especially effective for business-to-business mailings and back-end mailings for consumer products.

But for some sales letters — in particular those selling front-end information products to consumers who may not be familiar with your client's company — you will need to learn how to create a fourth kind of teaser ... one that promises a benefit in an unexpected way.

From Good to Great ... a Fourth Category

This fourth kind of teaser is one I learned from my partner, Bill Bonner, one of the great advertising copy masters of our time. He calls it "indirection." Here's how he explains it:

> When you write direct teasers, the prospect knows you are trying to sell her. She thinks, "I know what's going on here. I'm being sold." Alerting your prospect so directly to the sales pitch makes her more likely to refuse your offer. I prefer a more roundabout way of catching her interest by creating a statement or question that gets her thinking about something else — something that will lead to the sale, but not right away.

Back at the Explorers Society Party

Before I explain how the indirection teaser works, let's go back to the party. You are standing at the bar, trying to come up with an opening line, but you can't think of anything at all. Luckily your department head has given you the name and phone number of someone who can help you. He is an expert in meeting attractive women. One of his specialties is coming up with great opening lines.

His name is Mystery. He's the featured pick-up guru described in Neil Strauss's best-selling book *The Game: Penetrating the Secret Society of Pickup Artists* and starring in *The Pick-Up Artist*, the HBO reality show.

You make your way to the pay phone in the hallway, and phone Mystery. He is expecting your call.

"What lines have you thought of?" he asks?

You tell him: "Hi, I'm looking for a beautiful, intelligent woman to romance."

"Too narcissistic," he replies.

"How about 'I can make you rich and happy'?" you say.

"No! Too obvious. Too direct."

He tells you that the narcissistic lines will turn women off and predictable lines like "Can I buy you a drink?" or "Haven't I seen you somewhere before?" will make them feel defensive.

"She's here," Mystery says, "to have a good time and maybe meet a nice man. She knows that most guys out there are looking for a one-night stand. If you hit her with a line that makes her think, 'Oh, I know what this guy is up to,' you'll probably lose her."

A much better approach, Mystery says, is to walk up to the woman *next to* the one you're interested in and start a conversation with her.

"By engaging the other woman, you also engage the woman you're interested in ... but *indirectly*," he explains.

"She doesn't think you are particularly interested in her because you are talking to her friend. But if your opening line is compelling, she will be drawn into the conversation."

"I like that indirect approach," you tell Mystery. "But I'm still stuck for an opening line. What can I say?"

"I can't tell you that," he says. "It depends on the circumstances and on the lady in question. But I can give you some lines that have worked for me. One of them might work for you."

You are, of course, very interested. Mystery suggests five possibilities:

"Oh my God! Did you see those two women fighting outside?"

"I wonder if you could help me settle a debate?"

"Hey, looks like the party is over there."

"So, how do you two know each other?"

"Can I get your opinion on something?"

You scribble the lines down on a scrap of paper, thank Mystery for his help, and return to your place at the bar. The beautiful woman is still where she was, talking to her friend. You order another drink and study the lines Mystery has given you. They are, as he said, indirect. They have nothing to do with you or your intentions. In steering attention away from romance, they reduce the possibility of emotional resistance and allow for a more relaxed and enjoyable conversation.

Of the five lines Mystery has given, you like the second one best. You finish your drink, walk over to the two women, and address the older one. You say, "I wonder if you could help me settle a debate?"

Both women look at you inquisitively. There is not a trace of skepticism on their faces. The older woman smiles and says, "What's that?"

You reply, "A colleague of mine says that tribal amulets are just hocus pocus and can't have any real magical power. But I believe it is possible that they do. What do you think? Is there such a thing as magic?"

She ponders the question a moment, then replies, "I'm a scientist. I'm not a big believer in magic."

At which point her friend, the woman you want, chimes in. "I'm not so sure. I think anything is possible."

"You do?" you say, turning toward her. "So maybe you can clear up a mystery that's been troubling me for some time."

She seems flattered by your comment. You realize you've just used your advisor's name — a nod, no doubt, to his genius.

You continue. "I have brought back some very special amulets from Peru. The tribe that's been guarding them for thousands of years believe they have the power to bring good luck and ward off evil. When I liberated them ..."

"What do you mean by 'liberated'?" she says.

"Well," you say, affecting embarrassment. "These things are very rare. Very difficult to get hold of. In fact, the ones I have in my possession now might be the most valuable ever brought into this country."

She takes a half-step toward you. "Really? Tell me more ..."

Cut. Fast-forward 15 minutes.

"If you'd like, I could show them to you."

"Really? I think I would like that!"

"As it happens, they're just a few minutes from here — at my house."

"My car or yours?" she asks.

"Let's take my Land Rover," you reply. It's got a few years on it, but it rides as well as any new model."

She smiles widely. "I'm sure it does," she says.

By taking Mystery's advice, you have initiated a conversation that was not about you but about something you suspected she was interested in. (Why else would she be at the Explorers Society party?) Thus, the conversation moved quickly and easily. You were able to tempt her with the promise of letting her see your treasure. And you exposed some of your personality (admitting to the "liberation"), which she seemed to like.

By the time you suggested that the two of you move on to your house, she was pushing the action because she was thinking about what she wanted, not your intentions.

This brief, but effective approach worked so well, you realize, because you followed Mystery's advice and began with an indirect opening line that led to a brief, but intriguing conversation.

Getting back to our direct-mail sales letter, your indirect opening line ("I wonder if you could help me settle a debate?") is equivalent to the main part of an indirect teaser on the outer envelope, which is usually printed in large, bold type. And the little conversation that ensued is equivalent to the copy below the main part of the teaser.

Here's an example selling a Nightingale-Conant audiotape program:

Nightingale
◟Conant

PRESORT
STANDARD
U.S. POSTAGE
PAID
NIGHTINGALE-
CONANT

NO ONE gets rich without it.
But with it, people achieve the "impossible."

Donald Trump admits he needs one.
Bill Gates has one.
Oprah Winfrey has one too.
Henry Ford built an empire from it.
And it helped **Steven Spielberg.**

It's how they've all reached enormous heights of success and built massive wealth. It's also how you can build massive wealth and achieve impossible dreams — even if you lack time, money, or necessary skills. It's that powerful.

What is it? *Look INSIDE!*

This copy demonstrates the power of the indirect teaser. At a glance, the reader is challenged to guess what it is that "no one can get rich without." Her curiosity is piqued. And it is stoked by discovering that Donald Trump, Bill Gates, and other famous people "need" it or "have" it.

Instead of taking a direct approach (perhaps "Our Audiotape Program Is the Best in the World" or "Get Wealthy With This $39 Program"), the copywriter has opted to divert the reader by presenting the product's benefit indirectly, as a secret. The reader cannot resist the temptation to open the envelope.

Now, back at the party, your love interest takes your arm and you walk her to your "vintage" Land Rover. You exchange smiling glances of anticipation as you drive the short distance to your house. Your next challenge: Get her to step inside!

3

The Seduction: The Headline and Lead

The Three P's of the Headline and Lead

- **Purpose:** to get the prospect to read the rest of the sales letter so the sale can be made

- **Problem:** to overcome the fact that the prospect is looking for a reason to stop reading (A headline and lead that is dull or boring in any way will almost surely fail.)

- **Possibility:** to intensify the good feelings the prospect got from reading the envelope teaser (You want to confirm her hope that this letter is about something important and exciting – bring her to the point where she is thinking, "This is really good! I'm really glad I'm reading this!")

Where were we? Oh, yes. You have persuaded the young lady to come to your house by using an irresistible opening line that was supported by a brief but tantalizing conversation (something about showing her some ancient amulets you discovered on your last trip to Peru). In crafting that opening, you took care to do everything you had to do. You:

- Grabbed her attention

- Diverted her interest away from romance

- Implied a significant benefit in going home with you

Now you are in front of your house. You get out of the car, walk around to the other side, and open her door. She steps out and looks at the house. What impression should it make on her?

Should it look amazing? Like a mansion? Overwhelming? No. Rather, it should look like she expects it to look.

And what would that be?

Choosing the Right Look

Like your clothes, the front of your house should be consistent with the image you are trying to project — in this case, a house that Indiana Jones might live in.

In fact, your house is perfect for this. It is a smallish, ivy-covered cottage with clapboard walls and faded paint.

Your young lady looks at it and says, "What an interesting place!"

This is what happens when the prospect takes the contents from the envelope. At a glance, they must look

right. The quality and color of the paper and the type must be consistent with the emotional expectations created by the envelope.

Consistency is key. If the teaser suggests an upscale, exclusive offering, the contents of the envelope should look upscale and exclusive. If the teaser suggests an offering that is downscale and cheap, the elements of the package should look downscale and cheap.

The headline of the sales letter, too, should be consistent with what the prospect is expecting.

Robert Cialdini, in his book Influence: *The Psychology of Persuasion*, explains why consistency is so important when you're trying to persuade someone to do something:

> ... *in most circumstances consistency is valued and adaptive. Inconsistency is commonly thought to be an undesirable personality trait. The person whose beliefs, words, and deeds don't match may be seen as indecisive, confused, two-faced, or even mentally ill. On the other side, a high degree of consistency is normally associated with personal and intellectual strength. It is at the heart of logic, rationality, stability, and honesty.*

In responding emotionally to the teaser, your prospect has made an emotional commitment to take a look at what's inside the envelope. If the contents look, at a glance, to be consistent with what she expected from the teaser, she will read the headline. If the headline is emotionally different from what she is expecting, she will be disturbed. She will remember that she is being sold something, and will feel a little bit manipulated ... which will worry her.

So there you are, standing by your car with this woman looking at your house. She likes what she sees. It is consistent with her expectations. Now you have a choice. You can say nothing, just take her by the elbow and lead her in. Or you can say something like, "Well, shall we take a look at those amulets?"

By repeating — or nearly repeating — your opening line, you put her at ease. This is why most professional copywriters use headlines for their sales letters that replicate the idea of the teaser.

Choosing the Best Headline for the Sales Letter

The advantage of replicating the teaser as a headline on top of the sales letter may seem too obvious to mention. But many copywriters don't follow this logic. They write one teaser for the envelope, and another one as the headline. They probably think they are adding something extra to the package by doing so. And there is a chance that a different headline would do that. But the chance is very small. And the risk of losing the emotional feeling you've stirred up with the envelope teaser is very great.

So my advice is: Write a headline that reinforces the teaser. Let me give you some examples.

First, notice how, in the following copy from Nightingale-Conant, the headline copy mirrors the teaser copy.

Nightingale ✆ Conant

PRESORT
STANDARD
U.S. POSTAGE
PAID
NIGHTINGALE-
CONANT

NEW from Dr. David Hawkins!

Are you ready to go from merely believing in God to actually knowing the Divine exists?

INSIDE: Your opportunity to discover a
direct path to God that is known to only
the most serious spiritual devotees.

Notice how the word "Divine" is used in both the teaser and the headline. Also notice the related words that are used — *realization, realities, believing,* and *knowing.* Consistency.

Notice how the actual phrase "discover a Direct Path to God" is used in both the teaser and the headline. This is a great example of consistency.

Nightingale ✆ Conant

NEW from Dr. David Hawkins!

**Discover the
Direct Path to God**

This way of "being" in the world
removes the barriers to
Divine Realization and reveals the
magical divine realities that are
happening to you every day of your life

Dear Friend,

Now take a look at this package from the Health Sciences Institute (HSI) in Baltimore. It contains a letter explaining what you'll discover in this little bookalog. The sales pitch is also in the bookalog.

Both the envelope teaser and the bookalog title have the identical text.

The letter headline varies a bit by using "Natural" instead of "Forbidden." But the point is the same … "'they' won't let us have" is just another way of saying "Forbidden."

Also, there is a symbolic chain on both the bookalog and the envelope that represents the barrier to this coveted information.

Consistency!

Finally, let's look at an example of a sales package where the teaser and headline are completely different.

Study the piece for a while. Can you feel how emotionally different they are? Would it surprise you to know that this package failed?

I can't know for sure, but my guess is that copywriters sometimes do this because they have written more than one great teaser and they don't want to "lose" the one they decided was in second place. That's understandable. But the way to use that second-best teaser is to put it somewhere else. It could be a subhead somewhere later in the sales letter. Or it could be a headline for a lift note or brochure.

Back to our extended metaphor ...

By saying something to the young lady about seeing the amulets, you make it easier for her to enter your house. If, instead of reinforcing your opening line, you say something emotionally different ("Well, now let's get our clothes off and hop into my hot tub!"), there's a good chance she'll back out right then and there.

Making Your Headlines Emotionally Appropriate

The purpose of the headline, most copy experts say, is to get the prospect to read the sales letter. But that is not entirely true. If it were, almost any outrageous headline would do.

Great headlines — like great envelope teasers — do more work than that. They attract attention. They arouse curiosity. But they also must bring the prospect into the letter with the right emotional expectations (emotional expectations the copywriter will tap into later to sell the product).

Same thing is true in our extended metaphor: If the only purpose of what you say to the woman at the bar is to get her into your house, you could say pretty much anything that would work, including lying to her. But that's not your purpose. Your *purpose* is to bring her into your house with the right feelings. Why? Because you don't want a one-night stand, you want a relationship.

So if you are presenting yourself as Indiana Jones, your house should look like a house Indiana Jones might live in. If it looks like a frat house with toilet paper hanging from the trees and beer cans strewn all over the yard, she will think you are a fake and will turn around and run!

By mimicking your opening line as you walk her to the door, she will be thinking about the ostensible reason she is there — to look at those Peruvian amulets. Any skepticism or fear she might have had at this moment will be reduced.

But as she steps into the foyer and you close the door behind her, her skepticism will surely come to the surface. "Here I am alone in this stranger's house," she will think. "Does he really want to show me those amulets? Or does he have something else in mind?"

In bringing your love interest through the front door, you can't prevent her from feeling that way, just as you can't prevent a sales prospect from having a moment's hesitation as she starts to read your sales letter. What the lady is likely to think at that point is, "Okay. I'll give this guy just enough time to let me check out those amulets. If he tries anything funny, I'm out of here."

Starting the Seduction

Thus we come to the most sensitive part of any sales letter: the lead.

What is the lead?

It's the copy that comes after the headline. It includes the salutation and a certain amount of copy that follows.

How much copy? That depends on two things:

1. The strength and complexity of the headline — how deep the promise is

2. The length of the sales letter

When the prospect opens the envelope and pulls out the contents, she is motivated by some promise of a benefit that was stated or implied by the teaser and reinforced by the headline. If the promise is very simple ("Get a $100 Fountain Pen for the Price of a Postage Stamp"), she's not likely to give you a lot of time to make your case. If it's more complicated ("Make $65,233 a Month by Tapping Into Secret Government Funds"), she's likely to give you more time.

Likewise, if the sales letter is only four pages, she probably will make a read-or-toss decision by the middle of the first page. If it's 16 pages or more, she might commit to the middle of the second page.

I have never heard this suggested before, but I believe this is one of the reasons why long copy generally sells better than short copy. Long copy, however good or bad it is, gets a bigger commitment of time from the prospect and, therefore, gives the copywriter more space to try to accomplish the sale.

Although it takes up only a fraction of the total word count, the lead does the lion's share of the selling. You may be familiar with Pareto's 80-20 rule. It tells us that 80 percent of any objective is achieved with 20 percent of the available means. As applied to the sales letter, that means 80 percent of the selling is done in the lead, though it's typically no more than 20 percent of the copy.

A good headline will get your prospect to read the beginning of your sales letter — but not the entire thing. Remember, she has more mail to read than she has time to devote to it. She may be hoping that your letter will prove useful and interesting, but she isn't sure. She is somewhat skeptical. She will give your letter only a few minutes of her time to persuade her that she should continue to read. If you haven't sold her then, she'll toss it and go on to something else.

If your goal is to get the prospect to read more of your sales letter, you want to choose a headline that does the best job of attracting attention, creating a desire to read on, and reducing sales resistance. In most cases that means you should make the headline strong and complex and make the sales letter itself very substantial. In saying that, I don't want to suggest that complex headlines are always better (although they often are) or that longer copy is always better (although it usually is). I simply want to point out the psychological impact of those things. As a copywriter, you need to know it.

Let's go back to our metaphor.

You and your love interest have just stepped into the house and are now standing in the foyer. Like the lead, the foyer is small — perhaps the smallest room in the house. But instead of simply walking her through it quickly, your intuition tells you that you should linger there — that, if you are going to achieve your ultimate purpose, you need to make some important romantic gesture in the foyer.

You look at her. Her eyes are bright with expectation. She is happy to be there, eager to see the amulets.

You close the door and tell her to have a seat while you hang up her coat. On your way to the closet, you say (over your shoulder), "There's a book on the table next to you about amulets. I think you'll find it interesting."

"Oh, good!" she says. You glance back. She is engrossed in the book.

You have diverted her attention from your ultimate mission and focused it back on the reason she came with you. You haven't yet kept your promise — of showing her the Peruvian amulets — but you have catered to the same expectation by mentioning the book she is now reading.

You wait a while at the coat closet, giving her time to go through the book. You know that she will notice that you are its author. That will validate what you told her when she met you — that you are an expert in amulets. And it will make her trust you more, which can only make it easier to seduce her later.

The Language of Love

The experts documented in Neil Strauss's book *The Game* are very good at seduction but very bad at developing meaningful relationships with women. They are like technically proficient copywriters who know how to write powerful headlines that entice the prospect to read the sales letter, but can't write sales letters that initiate loyal, long-term customer relationships.

A-level copywriters understand and focus on the long-term goal. They know that a customer relationship that will be highly productive over time has to begin with authenticity and enthusiasm.

That means never making a promise that can't be kept. And writing in a voice that is authentic — that represents the company selling the product in a genuine way.

One of my favorite examples of a promotion that uses exactly the right voice is the "Trout Spoken Here" letter.

This letter is short but powerful, because it speaks directly to a very targeted audience. It does not waste any time getting to the point. Notice that the lead uses jargon to prove that the reader and the writer speak the same language … and share the same passion for fly-fishing.

Notice, too, how the copywriter uses emotion — talking about the "amiable form of an incurable madness" that is the love of fly-fishing. And he throws in a bonus, in a handwritten note right at the beginning. Unusual.

Trout Spoken Here.
Also Bass. Salmon. And Bonefish.

CRAZY FOR FLY-FISHING? SEND FOR YOUR

COMPLIMENTARY ISSUE OF FLY FISHERMAN --

THE BEST THERAPY FOR VICTIMS OF THE

"INCURABLE MADNESS" DESCRIBED BELOW.

There's no obligation. But will throw in a FREE CREEL if you accept our subscription offer.

Fellow Angler:

There's bait casting. There's spin fishing. And then there's fly fishing --

-- what Robert Traver (author of Anatomy of a Murder but best known to fishermen for his love affair with trout) called "one of the more amiable forms of an incurable madness."

  If the hairs on your neck tingle at the vision of a dusk-rising brown gently finning as he looks upstream for hors d'oeuvres, you've got the madness.

I know I do. I'm the Editor of FLY FISHERMAN. Like Robert Traver I fish because ...

"... in a world where most men seem to spend their lives doing things they hate, my fishing is at once an endless source of delight and an act of rebellion ...

"... because trout do not lie or cheat and cannot be bought or bribed or impressed by power, but respond only to quietude and humility and endless patience ..."

I've got it bad; this amiable madness. And so do all of us here at FLY FISHERMAN magazine.

When we're not hipdeep in New York's Beaverkill, Montana's Bighorn or California's Hat Creek, we're planning our next trip -- swapping stories about our last one -- or writing about it in FLY FISHERMAN.

It's important to remember that this young lady has her own agenda. She wasn't at that fancy bar at the Explorers Society party to put beer in her belly. She is looking for romance too. And her ideal boyfriend is someone smart, adventuresome, accomplished, and worldly. In fact, it's someone just like you!

On the one hand, she is fearful she that when she meets a man at a bar, even a fancy bar, he will want to trick her into a one-night stand. On the other hand, she does want a romantic relationship with the right sort of person. So the more you look like a suitable partner, the more excited she will become.

It's the same thing with a sales letter. Your prospect doesn't want to be duped into buying something she doesn't want, but that doesn't mean she doesn't want to buy. In fact, she loves to buy. And buys all the time..

Back in the foyer, your dream girl is looking around. On the table next to the book, she finds a stack of old photos — mementos from your adventures in Malaysia, Sri Lanka, and Tibet. On the wall above the table hang dust-covered awards you've received from various archeological organizations. A tattered copy of *National Geographic* magazine on the floor has a photo of you on the cover.

"Holy Cow!" she thinks. "This guy is the real deal."

This is exactly what you were hoping would happen — that she would sell herself on you while you were taking your time hanging up her coat.

Keep in mind that all those discoveries about your accomplishments took place while you were absent from the room. She found them herself by poking around. She has no idea you wanted her to see them — that, in fact, you planted them there. She came to your house, she believed, simply to see your Peruvian amulets. But now she knows that she wants something more. She wants access to the man who found those amulets!

By the time you come back into the foyer, smiling disarmingly and carrying a Singapore Sling made with her favorite gin (you paid attention at the bar), she has decided she wants you.

When you suggest that she follow you into the living room to "chat," she practically jumps out of her seat to get there.

That is what happens with a well-constructed lead. In the space of just a few hundred words, you can take your prospect from an emotional state of modest anticipation to an overwhelming feeling of positive expectation. By "positive expectation," I mean a feeling of strong conviction about the usefulness of what she's reading. It's a feeling I'm sure you've had many times. You think: "This is really good. I'm glad I'm reading this. I can't wait to read more!"

So that's the copywriting challenge: To raise your prospect's emotions up to that level. How can you do that? How can you ratchet up the feeling created in the headline to that level of excitement and intrigue?

The Categorical Imperative and the Strategy of Indirection

Of all the many copywriting techniques I learned from Bill Bonner, the most powerful was the strategy of indirection. I mentioned this in Chapter 2 when we were talking about writing great teasers. But it applies to headlines and leads too. In a training program we co-taught to a small group of young copywriters in the early 1990s, Bill described the reasoning behind the strategy something like this:

> *The mind is a filtering mechanism. It receives more data than it can process at any one time. To avoid being overloaded, it has mechanisms to sort and process new information. One of those methods was identified by Immanuel Kant many years ago. He called it the categorical imperative.*

> *To process new information efficiently, the mind wants to disregard or file away as much as it can as quickly as it can. If it recognizes something as a version of something it already knows, it "files" it quickly in that category. So if your copy looks like "advertising," it will file it mentally in the junk mail slot and ignore it.*

To prevent your prospect's brain from doing that, the copy-writer must write copy that is fresh and different and in some way unexpected. Above all, it must not sound like something the prospect has read before.

When you approach a copywriting challenge logically, the teasers and headlines and leads you create tend to be very direct, like "10 Reasons to Buy Our Milk" or "Buy My Investment Newsletter and Watch Your Portfolio Triple." There is nothing fundamentally wrong with direct teasers and headlines and leads. They arrest attention and stir desire. Yet they are likely to be viewed by the reader's brain as something she has seen before. And then they are filed away under the category copy must always avoid: junk mail.

When Bill and I first taught that program, I didn't recognize how important the strategy of indirection is. By that time, I had written lots of very successful sales letters with direct headlines and leads. They seemed to work as well as the less-direct copy Bill was famous for. I figured that he liked indirect headlines and leads because he saw himself as a subtle man. I had a rougher view of myself, so I tended toward direct copy. Neither was better, I thought. It was just a matter of style.

But over the years, I've changed my mind. Though I am still an advocate of direct headlines and leads for business-to-business and back-end offers, I now favor the indirect approach for front-end sales letters that sell information-oriented products.

The information business is unique. What you are selling is not a physical thing that can be measured objectively, but a quality of judgment and expertise that is more subjective. This subjectivity lends itself to long-term personal relationships that hinge on deep seated feelings and ideas about how the world works (or should work). Selling financial advice, for example, is not as simple as selling a history of investment performance. It is much more about selling the economic and potential world view of the person or institution giving the advice.

The same holds true for advice about health, education, morality, entrepreneurship, child rearing, pet care, etc. We all want to get that kind of information from someone who sees the world as we do.

This very human tendency — to want to get our information from people we trust — is the keystone that holds together everything else. When selling information products, every other copywriting technique depends on this. And that is why indirection is such a profound technique. It allows you to establish that trust without a great deal of resistance on the part of your prospect, and it sets a sturdy foundation on which to build a long-term relationship with her.

There is a second reason why I now prefer indirect headlines and leads for information products. I believe they result in deeper customer relationships and higher lifetime values.

That's what Bill and I discovered when we looked at the renewal rates of our newsletters.

Newsletters whose subscribers were brought in by very direct promises ("Make 300% on Tech Stocks Using My Special System") tended to have weaker renewal rates — particularly if the newsletter failed to deliver fully on the promise. ("I only made 250% last year. Cancel my subscription.")

But those whose subscribers were brought in through indirect headlines and leads ("The Plague of the Black Debt: How to Profit From the Government's Reckless Spending Spree") tended to renew at higher rates, even when the performance of investment recommendations made by the newsletter was negative!

That was a remarkable fact to consider. We were selling newsletters with the ostensible purpose of delivering profitable investment advice. And yet some of the newsletters that gave terrible advice were getting higher renewal rates — considerably higher renewal rates — than some of those that performed very well.

The difference lay in the subscribers themselves. Those who had been brought in by direct headlines and leads saw us as a marketing organization and were willing to buy our products because our promises were so strong. But they had no other connection to us. Those who had been brought in through indirect headlines and leads were expecting something else from us — something more subtle and complicated that would take years to deliver.

Understanding the Core Emotional Complex

This brings us to another useful principle of direct selling — one I developed many years ago and have been advocating ever since. I call it the *core emotional complex*. Like the strategy of indirection, it's a powerful tool that can transform B-level copy into A-level copy and put you in the ranks of the world's best copywriters.

To understand the core emotional complex — the subtle, underlying feelings and desires that motivate your prospect — we must bust another copywriting myth, the most common myth of all. It's this: When it comes to selling, there are only two emotions that count — greed and fear.

The greed-and-fear myth is so widely pronounced and believed that what I'm about to say might sound heretical. But here it is:

> *There are many useful emotions that can and should be used in writing copy. Greed and fear are two of them — but they are two of the crudest and most common emotions used and, therefore, among the least useful to employ when creating a headline and lead for your sales letter.*

The A-level copywriter knows this instinctively. He knows that envy and shame, for example, are stronger than greed or fear. Greed and fear are everywhere, parading in front of us like streetwalkers trying to figure out which pocket we keep our wallet in. But less-commonly employed emotions — like envy and shame — are more powerful precisely because they are less frequently used.

Let's take a look at some headlines and leads built around two other underutilized emotions: hidden pride and repressed anger.

This is a space ad from a magazine. It not only taps the underutilized emotion of hidden pride ("If you want to look like me, do what I did"), but also implies an additional benefit: self-confidence. Plus, it illustrates this woman's weight loss in a very effective way.

You see 10 watermelons on the table with a scale above — and that registers indelibly in your mind.

Here's a Nightingale-Conant headline and lead that touches on repressed anger. Many people are reaching out for a better way to grow old gracefully. They want to be healthier and are losing faith in traditional medicine. And this copy conveys hope, excitement, and assurance.

Nightingale
⊙ Conant

Stop being duped by so-called 'facts' and false propaganda about health, wellness, and aging!

Meet the renegade Ph.D. who has finally cracked the secrets of anti-aging and perfect health ...

and the revolutionary 7-step system he has created that is guaranteed to make you feel healthier, stronger, and — YES — younger ... today, tomorrow, and for the rest of your long, vibrant life!

Dear Friend,

How healthy do you want to be? How good do you want to look and feel? How long do you want to live?

Simple enough questions, right? After all, if you're like me and most everyone else, you want to be as healthy as possible ... look and feel as good as possible ... and live as long as possible.

Unfortunately, chances are also good you're not on track to achieving any of those things at this very moment.

That's because even if you're trying to eat right, exercise, and do all the things "they" tell you are good for you, the TRUTH about what causes good health and longevity (and what prevents them) is a well-kept secret — jealously protected by a whole collection of forces who profit by keeping you in the dark.

But don't worry! The purpose of this letter isn't to scare you. It's to let you know how easily this can change.

By committing to and applying seven simple steps, you can literally defy the chronological aging process and think, look, feel, and live younger now and for the rest of your long, healthy, vibrant life.

Skeptical? I can understand why. But if you're also intrigued, then I urge you to read on and find out how one man cracked the secrets of anti-aging ... what his amazing discoveries are ... and how they can transform, extend, and very possibly SAVE your life!

The problem with health in America

This is the cover of a seminar invitation.

If you know anything about receptionists and secretaries, you know the majority of them feel overworked ... underpaid ... and underappreciated. They don't feel their boss values them nearly enough. What receptionist would not want to be recognized as "Outstanding?"

Certainly repressed anger and hidden pride are evident here. But it makes the prospect feel that if she goes to this seminar she will learn the secret that will finally get her the attention and recognition she deserves.

The Outstanding Receptionist

Learn how to polish your image, perfect your telephone
skills, and increase your value to your organization.

Can you see how these examples are NOT about greed or fear? Can you see how they are appealing to emotions that are subtler and more complex?

If you want to create powerful headlines and leads, you must write copy that stimulates all sorts of emotions that lie beneath the surface.

This headline, for example, doesn't simply target the obvious (and very common) fear of public speaking, it touches on deeper feelings of self-consciousness and personal inadequacy:

Let me give you the secrets of
FEARLESS
CONVERSATION!

I promise you the ability to walk into a room full of strangers – and talk to <u>anyone</u> with total confidence, authority, and flair.

What never...<u>ever</u> to eat on an airplane!

The dirtiest, deadliest airline in the whole world

TRY IT FREE

- **How to get VIP treatment in hospitals. (All patients are <u>not</u> treated equally.)**
- **Cruise ship rapes: The uncensored facts which even the news media won't touch.**
- **How to find out if someone has a "past" — criminal record...bankruptcy...or whatever they're hiding.**
- **The little-known casinos in Atlantic City and Nevada that offer the best odds.**
- **Deduct the cost of your hobby as a business expense, even if you never show a profit.**
- **How to get an Oval Office tour of the White House.**
- **Get a hotel suite...while paying for a room.**
- **How competent/incompetent are your lawyer and accountant? Check 'em out...secretly.**

(And other surprising secrets you're not supposed to know.)

Dear Fellow American:

   This letter is about information that's "none of your business". For example...

   Did you know that certain specific foods they serve on planes will lower your blood sugar count at high altitudes -- leaving you tired... cramped...headachy?

   Now, perhaps you're thinking, "Why would airlines want to make me tired and grouchy?" Well, they don't want to, of course. But they <u>do</u> want to slice the cost of each meal -- so if it's cheaper, and (artificially) tastier...then -- why not?!!

   Let's talk about <u>survival</u>. You think, perhaps, that air safety is minutely scrutinized by the FAA...that all airlines regard careful

While this headline provokes fear, it also stirs curiosity. And as you read further, you can't help but wonder what all the secrets are.

The core emotion this example targets is the desire is to be more worldly and knowledgeable. Not only that, but the implication is that very few people have this information – which makes the reader feel that others will admire and envy her when they see how savvy she is.

What About Lust?

One of the odd things about the greed-and-fear myth is that the people who promote it have forgotten about the other gross emotion: lust. And lust is the one that's responsible for more selling than all the other emotions put together — including greed and fear.

Lust is responsible, or partly responsible, for trillions of dollars' worth of consumer sales every year. Lust perpetuates sales not just of romance fiction and pornography, but sales of cosmetics and jewelry and perfume and high-heeled shoes. Lust sells exercise videos, Viagra, luxury cars, and Victoria's Secret.

Why don't the greed-and-fear mythologists mention lust? Because for them, lust is useful only in selling sex. If they understood how lust works — the power of repressed lust — they would talk about it more.

Lust is a multibillion-dollar industry. Repressed lust is a trillion-dollar game.

Greed and Fear: The B-Level Copywriter's Mantra

Busting the greed-and-fear myth was an important step for me as a copywriter. It was the reason I was able to write my first breakthrough promotion (which launched the most successful newsletter franchise in the history of the industry). This is a secret that is as powerful as the secret of indirection, yet, like indirection, it has never been fully understood or widely used by copywriting gurus.

That is starting to change. Both indirection and the core emotional complex are part of the *American Writers & Artists Inc.* (AWAI) program and are being taught by a handful of master copywriters, including Paul Hollingshead, Don Mahoney, Mike Palmer, John Forde, and Bob Bly.

Still, when it comes to understanding their prospects' emotions, most copywriters are two-trick ponies, writing headlines and leads that are direct and conventional and that appeal to greed or fear.

Consider the following:

"Mysterious Government Fund Gives Some Investors Thousands Extra in Monthly Income."

What emotion is that headline evoking?

Yes, there is some greed there, but there is more than that. This headline is saying that if you read further, you will discover something you've always known — that the government is corrupt and given to taking from the poor and giving to the rich. The prospect who responds to that headline is not interested so much in getting hold of those dollars as she is in finding out what sneaky business the government is up to now and vindicating her long-held suspicions in the most concrete way possible: by getting on the good end of the cash flow!

To interpret that headline as greed-based is to grossly misunderstand and underestimate the prospect's motivations. A copywriter who follows that headline with a lead that is about the money ("Imagine what you could do with a few thousand extra dollars per month ...") rather than the intrigue ("I want to tell you about a secret division of the IRS that has, for more than 40 years, been siphoning off billions of dollars from ...") will wreck his chances of starting a highly profitable, long-term relationship with the customer.

The idea behind the core emotional complex is this: Human beings are not simple creatures. Our feelings are complicated, our thoughts fleeting, and our desires deep. When we make decisions, they are based on a combination of complicated feelings, fleeting thoughts, and deep desires. *If you can understand those feelings, thoughts, and desires and create a lead that binds them together with a single emotional string, you will have a powerful, breakthrough promotion.*

In *Influence: The Psychology of Persuasion*, Robert Cialdini identifies these psychological instincts that he says have a powerful influence on buying decisions:

1. Reciprocity — a feeling of moral obligation, a psychological burden we feel when we have been given an unasked-for kindness. Marketers often take advantage of this emotion by giving their prospects a "present" (an object or a bit of useful information) before asking them to buy their product.

2. Commitment to Consistency — a desire to feel that our actions are consistent with a higher code of behavior. Marketers tap into this emotion to help customers rationalize making the decision to buy.

3. Social Proof — the desire to buy things because of what other people, usually similar to us, have bought. This often determines which restaurants, movies, cars, etc. we choose. It is also why testimonials can be so effective in a sales letter.

The Interaction of Feelings and Desires

To get you thinking more about core emotions, here are some facts about human nature that A-level copywriters routinely keep in mind when they write sales letters.

- **Curiosity.** Everybody likes a good mystery, especially if it concerns a topic that is interesting to them for other reasons.

- **The Desire to Be Altruistic.** The desire to do good for others is based on a very deep, very pragmatic social truth. We all want the opportunity to act benevolently in certain situations. This is especially so when we feel guilty about having garnered more than our share of the good things life has to offer. Sometimes that can be a powerful motivating force in buying.

- **The Feeling of Loneliness.** Loneliness is a bad feeling, and for very good reasons. Evolution has hard-wired us to feel that survival is more likely with a little help from some friends. Inviting your prospect to come into a community of like-minded souls can be very compelling if it is done gracefully.

- **The Desire for Social Status.** How could the greed-and-fear mongers neglect this powerful emotion? How could they explain $20,000 watches, $200,000 cars, and $20 million homes based on greed or fear?

- **Exasperation and/or Defeat.** Who hasn't felt the frustration of failing to solve a persistent problem? Chronic back pain. An improper charge on a credit card that won't go away. The slow-moving carpenter who can't seem to finish the job. Such feelings beget desires for new solutions. Many great sales letters have taken advantage of this.

If this were a book about the core emotional complex, I could write 100 pages on such feelings and desires. But our purpose here is to learn how to write powerful headlines and leads. So let's stop here and make some observations.

Look at the above list again. Notice that those feelings and desires are often reciprocal. The feeling of loneliness, for example, is often accompanied by the desire for fraternity. Likewise, the feeling of guilt is often accompanied by a desire to be altruistic. (If this were not so, the non-profit fundraising industry would be a fraction of its current size.)

Notice, too, that most of those emotions are difficult to satisfy. Is it possible, for example, to eradicate the loneliness someone feels if they were abandoned by their parents at an early age? And if you were a victim of racism or social prejudice in your youth, how much social status would be enough to make you feel restored?

But that's a good thing. Because those desires can never be truly satisfied, it gives you the opportunity to talk to your prospects — and bond with them — at a deeper level. On the surface, you may be selling an electric juicer. But beneath that, you are giving your prospects a chance to atone for their self-destructive indiscretions (dietary and otherwise).

Be Careful About Negative Feelings

There's something else I want to point out abut those un-quenchable desires: The feelings that create them are negative. They tend to fall into one of two categories:

    1. Hurt ("I never got as much as I deserve.")
    2. Shame ("I have more than I deserve.")

This is important. These negative feelings are powerful. But *it is a big mistake to bring them up directly.*

I learned that early in my copywriting career when I wrote headlines that addressed these feelings in an obvious way.

    Are you embarrassed because you look fat?

    Are you ashamed of how rich you are?

    Are you tired of being lonely?

These efforts failed. For a while, I didn't know why. Then one day a friend asked me a similarly direct question. It was something like "Are you ashamed of yourself for being so mean to Larry at the meeting yesterday?"

My immediate reaction was to deny it. "No, I'm not ashamed," I said. "In fact, it was Larry who started it when he ... blah ... blah ... blah."

I knew I was lying. And I was lying because I was, indeed, ashamed. But I didn't want to talk about my shame. I knew that my friend had just given me an opportunity to get over my em-barrassment, but I couldn't summon the courage to take advan-tage of it.

Had he been more discrete, though, the conversation might have gone like this:

"Boy, Larry can really say some exasperating things, can't he?"

"Yes. Especially when he doesn't know what he's talking about."

"Well, you certainly put him in his place."

"Yeah, but I feel sort of embarrassed for doing it in such a mean way."

"How else could you have handled it?"

Thus, he would have put me exactly where I needed to be — in terms of my feelings and desires — to deliver the message that he needed to deliver and I needed to hear.

Read that interchange again and notice what happened. When my friend addressed my deeper feeling of shame directly, I denied it and subverted the conversation. When he was indirect, he achieved his purpose very effectively. Because then I was the one putting a name on my own negative emotions.

That's why, when creating your headline and lead, you should not *name* the negative feelings you're evoking. It's much better to get to them at an angle, by saying something assuring that the prospect can agree with. And then, by a series of carefully guided psychological prompts (which you, as the copywriter, control), lead her to the feelings and desires that you need her to respond to so you can sell her your product!

Great sales letters don't tell the customer what to think … or feel … or want. They locate the prospect's feelings, thoughts, and desires, and then stimulate them. They provoke the prospect to do the feeling and thinking on her own. In taking this indirect approach, you avoid the possibility that your prospect will take refuge in denial, and give her a chance to follow the course of her own feelings.

I know, I know, I've strayed from our archeology professor metaphor. But what I've just described is, metaphorically speaking, like leaving your lover in the foyer and letting her look around at all those seemingly haphazard (but actually planted) props that lead her to conclude, on her own: "This is the Indiana Jones of my dreams!"

Thoughts Matter Too!

The core emotional complex is a bundle of the prospect's deeper feelings, thoughts, and desires tied up with an emotional cord. We have looked at how feelings and desires interact, but we have said nothing yet about thoughts.

Some advertising gurus will tell you that what the customer thinks doesn't matter. People buy things for emotional reasons, they argue, so make the pitch entirely emotional. There is an element of truth to that, but it is fundamentally misleading. Feelings and desires are two-thirds of the core emotional complex, but thought is the other third ... and thought matters.

If you are selling rare U.S. coins to investment newsletter subscribers, for example, it pays to know what they think about collectible coins in general and the type of coins you are selling in particular. If you know, for example, that they have been barraged by articles in their newsletter that are predicting an escalation in the value of gold, then it is likely they believe rare coins are good investments. But if they have been reading a lot about fraud in the collectibles arena, they may be thinking otherwise — that buying coins is a risky business.

I am talking about thoughts here, not feelings. Thoughts are often connected to feelings ("I think that coins are risky investments, therefore I feel nervous about buying them."), but they are not feelings and need to be handled differently.

Feelings — especially negative feelings, as we've just seen — must be dealt with indirectly. But thoughts *can* and *should* be handled head-on.

Going back to our rare coin example, you could address the thought of coins being risky investments by saying, "Think coins are risky? Listen to this..."

Imagining the Heart and Mind

Before you begin writing a sales letter, you need to take an inventory of all the feelings, thoughts, and desires that your prospective buyer is likely to have relative to the product you are selling. You can do that by asking yourself the following questions:

- When the prospect first reads this letter, where will she will most likely be? In her home? In her office?

- What time of day will it be?

- Will she be relaxed or tense?

- How many other sales letters is she likely to be looking at then?

- Relative to this product, what are her biggest fears?

- Relative to this product, what are her current thoughts?

- What negative feelings might she have about this subject?

- Considering her thoughts and feelings, what are her desires?

- Which of those desires has frustrated her the most?

Don't just list one thought, feeling, and desire. Take some time. Exhaust the possibilities. The purpose of this exercise is to get you to think more deeply about your prospect's core complex. If you can figure out that, then you can write a stronger and more compelling sales letter.

Once you have answers to all of the above questions, study them. Imagine the prospect receiving your sales letter. Try to visualize it. How big is the headline? What does it say? Imagine the prospect reacting to the headlines that suggest themselves to you. Now ask yourself: "What is she feeling? What is she thinking? What does she want?"

This process — this exercise in sympathetic imagination — is the single most important part of the creative process of copywriting. Getting a bead on your customer's heart and mind is the only way to write exceptional copy. B-level copywriters can create decent packages by using all the tricks and techniques that B-level copywriting gurus teach. But it is impossible to compete successfully in the six-figure A league unless you can write headlines and leads that connect with the prospect in a deep way.

The Golden Thread

There is no exact process you can follow to discover the core emotional complex. The best you can do is conjure up a list of possible feelings, thoughts, and desires and then spend some time trying them on, one at a time.

When you've hit one that feels right — one that gets you more excited than the others — trust your instinct and go with that.

Write a sentence or two that encapsulates that core complex. You can use that sentence as your headline, as a subhead, or simply as a tool to remind you of the core complex. That sentence — if it's well-crafted — will incorporate the key feelings, thoughts, and desires that you've identified as important. If it does incorporate them, it will stimulate a particular emotion in you each time you say it. That emotion will be a complicated one — one you won't be able to put a name to — precisely because it represents a complex of feelings, thoughts, and desires.

Imagine this sentence as a group of powerful golden batteries. And imagine your copy as a wire that is connected from this battery pack to your prospect. If the core complex is strong, it will generate a great deal of current. Enough to charge her up with excitement every moment she is reading your sales letter.

Every sentence you write should be connected to this golden battery pack. Every paragraph should be charged with strong emotion. If it is not, you must cut it out. The current must always be running or the letter will fail.

I have been teaching the secret of the core emotional complex for about 15 years. I have written about it a dozen times, explained it that many times at seminars, and incorporated it into the AWAI copywriting program. It would not be an exaggeration to say that thousands of copywriters and copywriting students have been exposed to it. Yet there are probably fewer than a dozen copywriters today who incorporate this concept into their writing.

It amazes me. And I suppose it should depress me. But it doesn't. Because the less this secret is used, the more power it has when it is deployed. That's good for the good guys. Master indirectness and the core emotional complex and you will be a master copywriter. Ignore them and you will have to be satisfied with getting mediocre results by using the tricks and gimmicks that crowd the pages of most books on copywriting.

What the Lead Must Accomplish

I said that mastering the core emotional complex will put you way ahead of your copywriting colleagues. And that's true. But that's assuming you understand the architecture of a good lead. If you don't know how to put a good lead together, the advanced stuff won't help you.

Just in case you are unsure of how to structure a lead, let's review the basics.

The purpose of the lead is to get the prospect emotionally committed to read the rest of the sales letter. By the time she gets to the end of the lead, she needs to have this sort of thought in her head: "This is good! Really good! I'm glad I'm reading this!"

That's what you're shooting for — that level of excitement. But this isn't the only thing you have to accomplish with the lead. The purpose of your sales letter is to sell something. That means you have to link that enthusiasm to an expectation of benefit, one that will be provided temporarily by reading the sales letter ... and ultimately by buying the product.

But it all depends on having a strong lead. Because a strong lead does the hard work of making the emotional sale. If you make that sale by touching on the prospect's deepest feelings, thoughts, and desires, then the sales letter will generate a very strong response.

Great leads have some or all of the following characteristics. They:

- Maintain the attention that the teaser and headline attracted

- Convert that attention into a "diverting" thought process

- State or imply an immediate benefit

- Indirectly promise a deeper benefit

- Identify and defuse any negative thoughts

- Indirectly (subtly) evoke a negative feeling

- By evoking that negative feeling, stimulate a positive desire

- Heighten that desire to an irresistible level

All of that must be done in a very short amount of time — the two or three minutes of attention a good lead can demand.

Let's take a look at how one copywriter did it. The following excerpts were taken from a promotion selling Dr. Al Sears' newsletter, **Health Confidential For Men**, which starts out with the following teaser and headline:

Teaser: "It's A Lot of Bull! Don't Believe What You've Been Told About Your Health…"

Headline: "So much of what the medical establishment tells you is pure Bull"

- Maintain the attention that the teaser and headline attracted:

> "Eat less meat"
> "Cut out the butter and eggs"
> "Aerobics 'till you drop"
> "Take these drugs"
> "Don't smoke, drink, or have fun?"

- Convert that attention into a "diverting" thought process:

"Modern Politically Correct Medicine Is Trying To Turn You Into A Woman!"

- State or imply an immediate benefit:

"Here's the good news…"

- Indirectly promise a deeper benefit:

"So let other people follow the crowd and starve themselves eating bibs of lettuce, bland vegetables and tofu. Let them avoid meat, stop drinking beer and wine and the occasional shot of excellent Scotch and smoking a fine cigar, let them spend an hour a day on the treadmill, avoid sunshine and everything else that makes life fun and pleasurable…

Let them. God bless 'em. But you can forget all that nonsense."

- Identify and defuse any negative thoughts:

    "And turn yourself into a lean, muscle-packed man with the energy and sexual vitality of a 20-year old.

    How can I promise you this? Contrary to what most doctors and "health experts" say? Because none of these doctors and "health experts" have tackled the real questions:"

- Indirectly (subtly) evoke a negative feeling:

    "What are the primary factors of male aging? What can be done to correct age-related deterioration, deficiencies, and disease? The truth may startle you. The current treatments, theories and medicines may outrage you."

- By evoking that negative feeling, stimulate a positive desire:

    "Right here...right now...I'm going to tackle the myths, misconceptions and lies. And I'll tell you exactly what you can do to reverse the aging process in your body, and restore your health to what it was when you were young."

- Heighten that desire to an irresistible level:

    "In fact, it's very possible that with the information you're going to get today, you may now enjoy better health, conditioning, energy, and sexual vitality than you've ever had in your life."

A 12-Step Process for Writing Great Leads

Checking your leads against the above list of eight characteristics that great leads should have will help you identify strengths and weaknesses in the copy you write. Here's another list that will help you.

To get your leads written quickly and well, you might follow this protocol:

1. Make a list of every possible feeling that your prospects might feel in relation to the product.

2. Rate them in terms of intensity.

3. Identify one or two that you will focus on in the lead.

4. For that one or two, identify a reciprocal desire.

5. Write another list of any preconceived ideas (thoughts) that your prospects might have about the product you are selling.

6. For each negative idea, write a positive response.

7. Based on all of this, begin writing leads. Keep writing until you have three that you feel are very good.

8. Ask two or three colleagues to rate those leads on a scale of 1 to 4, with 1 being "I wouldn't read the sales letter" and 4 being "I would read the sales letter with a high degree of interest."

9. Select one of your leads that had an average score of 3 or above. (If none did, restart the process.) This is your lead for your sales letter. It is also the golden thread that is connected to the core emotional complex you arrived at by thinking about your prospect's feelings, thoughts, and desires.

10. Using the golden thread to guide you, keep working on your lead until you feel like you have written the best one you possibly can.

11. If the lead is longer than it should be (longer than a page and half for the typical sales letter), edit it down. Remember, the key thing about the lead is that it has to accomplish its mission within the brief period of time the reader will give it.

12. Once the lead is fit and polished, put it through the same review process as before. In this case, 1 would be "I wouldn't keep reading," while 4 would be "This is good. This is really good! I'm glad I'm reading this sales letter!" Keep working on the lead until you have achieved an average score of at least 3.2. The higher, the better.

Okay. Now let's get back to our metaphor. We meet up with you — our Indiana Jones-type archeology professor — as you are about to lead your lady out of your foyer and into the living room.

4

The Living Room: The Sales Argument

The Three P's of the Sales Argument

- **Purpose:** to get the prospect to feel that buying the product is the right thing to do

- **Problem:** to present all sorts of benefits, claims, and proof — but to do it without making the prospect feel confused, skeptical, or bored

- **Possibility:** to show the prospect that buying the product is the *rational* thing to do

---

As you lead your love interest into the living room, you walk confidently because you have seen the stars in her eyes.

You have won her heart. But you are not done yet. There are two more challenges that face you: You must win her mind. And then you must consummate the relationship.

The End Game

I have said that 80 percent of the success of a direct-response sales letter depends on the lead, which comprises only about 20 percent of the letter's length. The rest of the sales letter, it stands to reason, does only 20 percent of the work. But that work is important.

The lead is where you get the prospect to fall in love with your sales letter. It is where you get her to think, "This is really good! I'm very glad I'm reading this!"

But getting your prospect to fall in love with your sales letter is not enough. The end game is to get a *direct response* from her. To get that direct response, you have to retarget your copy from the prospect's heart to her brain. You have to answer any and all questions that might come to her mind after her heart has said "I'm sold."

There is no generally agreed upon way of referring to this next part of the sales letter. I like to call it the *sales argument*, because, like an argument you might make for a speech class, it is full of claims and proofs.

The sales argument begins where the lead ends, and continues until you have satisfied the prospect's mind that she is about to make a smart and sensible decision.

Why Stop in the Living Room?

Having noticed that the lady's pulse is racing, a less prudent lover would have taken her by the hand and walked her directly through the living room and straight upstairs to the bedroom. But you are not looking for a one-night stand. And you know that the moment she sees the stairs she will hesitate. She has been in this situation before. She has been disappointed before. She is hoping this time it will be different. You do too.

You know that if you ignore her concerns and use your overwhelming charm to get her upstairs at this point, you will have damaged the relationship a little. You want her to understand your good intentions. You want her to recognize all the value that you will be bringing to the relationship.

You need time to explain these things to her. And to answer any questions she might have about you and your intentions.

The 5 Copy Parts of a Typical Sales Letter

1. The Envelope Teaser

2. The Headline

3. The Lead Copy

4. The Sales Argument

5. The Closing Copy

So you invite her to sit down, sip her drink, and chat. There is so much you want to tell her. And so much you want to know about her too.

This is just what you should be doing when you write the sales argument. You know that you have captured your prospect's heart. But you want to assure her that she is about to make the right decision.

A strong lead will stir deep emotions. When emotions are swirling, the mind is saying, "Slow down and let me sort things out!"

The trick to writing a great sales argument is to satisfy the mind without losing the heart. Properly constructed, the sales argument should supply all the facts needed for your prospect to make a logical decision while, at the same time, keeping alive the strong feeling created in the lead.

The sales argument is where you repeat the big promise a dozen different ways, where you break it down into specific claims, where you prove those claims convincingly, where you introduce a big idea (if your sales letter has one), where you employ social proof (i.e., testimonials, endorsements, survey statistics, etc.) to demonstrate credibility, and where you ask and answer every important question your prospect might have about the product.

The sales argument is where you help your prospect think about how this new relationship will benefit her and talk frankly about all the risks and rewards, the benefits and drawbacks.

Promises, Claims, and Proof — the Elements of a Well-Crafted Sales Argument

The primary content of a well-crafted sales argument is an artfully sequenced arrangement of *promises*, *claims*, and *proof*. Interlaced between these elements are *stories*, *secrets*, *testimonials*, and *statements* — all of which add up to an airtight argument that buying the product is exactly the right thing for the prospect to do at that very moment in time.

If the product is good, it is easy to write this part of the sales letter. A good product has some fundamental quality that distinguishes it from its competition. This quality — its *unique selling proposition* (USP) — should be an important part of the sales argument. But it may not be the most important part. You may find that you want to emphasize some other characteristic of the product, some quality that is not unique yet fits better with the big promise you made in the lead.

If you do emphasize some other quality or characteristic of the product, it is still a good idea to articulate the USP toward the end of the sales argument. This is especially true if the cost of the product is higher than that of some other, similar products in the marketplace. Your prospect will want to rationalize her decision to pay more. There is no better way to do that than by identifying a USP.

Aside from a strong USP, a good product will usually have measurable benefits. And laudatory testimonials. And secrets too — reasons why it is as good as you say it is. There is a lot that can be said in favor of good products. And that's exactly what you must do in the body of the letter: Say almost every good thing you can think of.

You don't have to shout. You don't have to brag. (In fact, it's better if you don't.) But you do have to get all that good evidence out there. The prospect, excited by the lead, will be happy to keep reading so long as you repeat your promises, make new claims, and prove to her that all those promises and claims are valid.

Your prospect wants the relationship to continue just as much as you do. You just have to convince her that she isn't being duped.

As our archeology professor, you are well prepared for this conversation with your lady love. You are aware of all the little clues that she "discovered" in the foyer. Now is your time to explain them in more detail. And provide her with other reasons to be happy with you.

She wants you to give her a very good reason to keep trusting in you. Give it to her and she'll do whatever you ask. At this point, she's almost certain she wants you ... that you're the man she's been hoping and searching for. (When you make this assumption in your sales argument — and understand it — you'll become less of a salesperson and more of a persuader.)

During your time together in the living room, you will tell her more stories, show her more trophies, give her copies of some of your books, and so on. And you will answer every question about you that might come to her mind. You want her to be 100 percent certain that she has found the right man.

Yes, there's a lot to talk about before you climb that staircase to the bedroom. So you sit down, sip your drinks, and talk.

Promises, Promises

There is nothing more fundamental in sales copy than the promise. It is the basic statement of your intention: What you intend to do for the customer in return for the money she will be investing. Promises can be big or small, direct or implied.

Examples of Big Promises:

1. Grow <u>Twice</u> The Garden for <u>Half</u> The Cost

2. You Can Be Active & More Mobile in Just 10 Days!

3. Three Weeks To A Slimmer, Sexier Body!

4. How you can make $4,000.00 a day, sitting at your kitchen table, in your underwear!

Examples of Small Promises:

1. How to make bottled horseradish taste like the fresh kind.

2. Soothe a sore throat with Hershey's® Syrup

3. 3 safest places to hide your valuables

Examples of Direct Promises:

1. Triple your sales income within 12 months

2. Earn More Than 8X The National Average With Your Orange Savings Account

3. How to Keep Your Money from Being Murdered!

Examples of Implied Promises:

1. Forbidden Cures! Remarkable cures CENSORED by knife-happy surgeons and greedy drug companies!

   Medically proven remedies that heal *without* drugs or therapy!

2. This discovery made Finnegan a rich man. He quit his job and became a multi-millionaire, practically overnight.

3. There's a New Railroad Across America, And it's making some people very rich ...

The promises you make depend on the product you are selling, the circumstances of the sale, and the thoughts, feelings, and desires of your prospective customer. Masterful sales promotions usually consist of one main promise and several minor ones that derive from the main promise.

For example, take a look at this promotion for one of *PREVENTION*'s Health Books for Women.

PREVENTION 33 E. Minor St.
Emmaus, PA 18098

*************************** ECRLOT ** R-005

* **Please reply promptly.**
We can hold your spot as a
TEST PILOT until the deadline,
then we must offer it to the
next person on the list:

January 20, 2001

Dear

My name is **Catherine Cassidy.** I am the Editor-in-Chief at *PREVENTION* magazine. I'm
writing to you today to invite you to **"Test Pilot"** a new weight-loss program we
created just for women...

...The name of the program is **Banish Your Belly, Butt & Thighs Forever.** It is
a revolutionary new program for rapid weight loss and improved health.

The results I have seen with women who have already tested the Program are
amazing. Now, you're invited to enjoy the same results...

<u>Come "Test Pilot" our new Program for 21 days —</u>
<u>ABSOLUTELY FREE</u>!

When you test pilot the Program, you receive a copy of the just-released publi-
cation **Banish Your Belly, Butt & Thighs Forever.** It brings you all you need to
lose weight, flatten your stomach, trim your thighs and reduce your rear. It is
yours to review for 21 days without cost or obligation. You also receive a FREE
"THANK-YOU" GIFT, just for accepting this invitation.

Here are some important facts about the Program you should know:

FACT #1: The Program works **fast.** You will start to lose weight almost <u>immedi-</u>
<u>ately</u>. Your stomach will shrink. Your thighs will get tighter. Your backside
will "lift." In just 21 days your whole body will look leaner, fitter, sexier.

FACT #2: The Program is <u>unique</u>. When you open your package from **Banish Your**
Belly, Butt & Thighs Forever you'll notice that it is <u>unlike anything you've</u>
<u>ever seen</u> in at least two important ways:

1. <u>It blasts away fat from the specific areas of your body that "collect" fat.</u>
You'll discover <u>new methods</u> that "release" extra fat from your stomach, hips,
thighs, and bottom — even if you never could before.

2. <u>You'll see that your success is literally ensured — because it's **easy and**</u>
it's fun. You are <u>never</u> required to do anything unpleasant. That means <u>no</u> carrot
sticks (unless you want them!)... no hard exercise (unless you want to!)... <u>no</u>
giving up your favorite foods (I know you don't want to do that!). And, as
unbelievable as it sounds, this Program is fun. Yes, you read it right — <u>fun</u>. Fun
is the secret that keeps your motivation high: and speeds up your results!

<u>over, please</u>

Big Promise:
You'll lose
weight quickly
and your health
will improve.

Small Promises:
In addition to
quickly losing
weight, you'll
be toning those
"tough spots"
like your abs
and thighs.
(Notice the dif-
ference between
this and a big,
overriding idea
like "Experi-
ence Rapid
Weight Loss
and Improved
Health.")

Direct Promise:
21 days from
now, you'll have
the lean, toned
sexy body,
you've always
wanted (It's
specific, and
spells out the
benefits.)

Small Promise: If you follow this program
it's going to be easy and fun.

Claims

Claims are statements that support your promises.

Suppose you're selling a vacuum cleaner. Let's see how that works …

Promise: "You'll save time and energy."

Supporting claim: "Our supercharged motor jet-propels this machine over the thickest carpets."

Another supporting claim: "So lightweight you can run it up and down the steps with one hand."

Yet another supporting claim: "No bags to change. Nothing to assemble. Ready to go to work for you right out of the box."

Proof

You not only need to make claims to support your promises, you also need to back up your claims with proof. If the claims themselves are not proven, your promises collapse like a house of cards.

This is where many copywriters — even experienced copywriters — fall short. The promises are there. The claims are there. But the proof is spotty or lacking entirely.

Proof means proof — evidence that makes the claim believable. There are many ways of proving a claim:

- You can cite a scientific study.
- You can make a logical argument.
- You can quote an expert or authority.
- You can state a compelling fact.
- You can provide a testimonial.

- You can even "prove" a claim by using an analogy — a comparison between what you are claiming and some similar pattern in some unrelated area that the prospect is likely to understand and accept as true.

In the case of our vacuum cleaner example, you might provide the following types of proof:

Scientific study: According to the Vacuum Industry Council, it takes the average housewife 1.2 hours to thoroughly vacuum her house. By comparison, our customers report getting the job done in 38 minutes.

Logical argument: It just doesn't make sense to use anything but the best equipment for any job.

Authoritative citation: *Consumer Reports* labeled our vacuum a "Best Buy."

Statement of fact: Our vacuum weighs only 3.2 pounds.

Testimonial: *"What a difference! I've never been prouder of the way my house looks!"* — Sally Thompson, Green Lake, WI

Analogy: Like a tornado attacking everything in its path, our high-powered pump creates a vacuum that sucks up dust mites and microbes you can't even see.

How Much Proof Do You Need?

Here's a useful technique that will help ensure that your copy has all the proof it needs. After completing a draft of the sales argument, go back and highlight or underline every promise and every claim. Then look for a supportive claim or two for every promise and a proof or two for every claim. If you can't find them, go back to your product research and keep digging till you get what you need. If you can't, you should consider omitting the unsupported promise or claim.

You don't need to present all the claims and proof in a logical, linear way. In fact, it's better if they are more artfully employed. And keep in mind that what you are trying to do is employ a variety of proofs: studies, facts, endorsements, testimonials, and analogies. Establishing proof in such a varied way will give your promise more natural authority. The sales argument will seem less orchestrated.

Take a look at the following two examples to see what I mean — how promises, claims, and proof can work effectively and naturally throughout the sales argument.

First, from a sales letter for *The Pinchot Retirement Plan* ...

Wisconsin Paper Mill Worker uses "Pinchot Retirement Plan" to collect $18,850 in one day

There's a new way to retire worry-free in America.

Instead of working well into their 50s and 60s, a small group of Americans have discovered a unique "Retirement Plan" (made possible by a former Governor and U.S. Presidential Advisor), which could pay you thousands of extra dollars per month, no matter what your age or income.

The Los Angeles Times says to consider it if you are "looking for an investment that keeps growing, regardless of recessions or stock market turmoil."

Dear Reader,

For most people, August 7, 2006 was a day just like any other.

But for 55-year-old Ron Hanson, it was a morning he'll never forget.

While most of us were preparing our morning coffee, Hanson (a Madison, Wisconsin native who spent most of his career in the paper industry), was cashing a check worth $18,850, according to U.S. Gov't. records. That's more than most Americans earn in several months.

Incredibly... Hanson was not the only one pocketing an enormous payment that day—nor did he collect the largest check. Government records report:

- Arthur Simms from Minnesota received payment the very same day—a check for $2,865.20

- And Eugene Allen from Washington cashed a check for more than most Americans earn in an entire year: $108,832.

Why are these men receiving so much money?

Headline

Lead

Indirect Promise — The reader is intrigued by some novel way to get a lot of cash in a single day. He wants to read on to see what the "Pinchot Retirement Plan" is about.

Claim — The subhead asserts that the Pinchot Plan is new. This excites the reader and makes her wonder, "Why haven't I heard about this before?"

2nd Claim — People are already using this. It must be real.

3rd Claim — The plan was initiated by a congressman. That can be verified. This must be real.

4th Claim — An endorsement from a credible source makes yet another claim: This plan is unaffected by market swings.

Story Lead — very appropriate for an indirect headline.

1st Proof — Already, in the lead, we have the first proof, validating the $18,850 claim.

2nd and 3rd Proofs — support for the 2nd claim that others are already taking advantage of this "new" plan.

5th Claim — This tells the prospect that the plan is "perfect" for her.

In short, thanks to several U.S. government programs spearheaded by a lifelong Presidential Advisor and State Governor named Gifford Pinchot, you can now collect tremendous amounts of income, every single month of the year, without doing any extra work.

Called the "Pinchot Retirement Plan" by many participants, this program is perfect for retirees, folks who want to retire soon, or anyone who wants more money deposited into their bank account on a regular basis...

Lead

2nd Promise — This one is direct. Copy switches from third-person to second-person ("you").

Proof of the 5th Claim — that the plan is perfect for investors.

- As a fellow named Paul Lyons told *Forbes Magazine*: "I own a lot of stocks and bonds, but I don't think there's anything in the world you can invest in as good as [The Pinchot Plan]." (Paul Lyons original $500 stake is now worth more than $500,000.)

- That's why *Forbes* says it's: "Like owning an oil reservoir that gets bigger every year."

Beginning of Sales Argument

6th Claim and Proof — This is an analogy. Since it's also a quotation from a credible magazine, it's both a claim and a proof of claim in a single sentence!

7th Claim and Proof — Now another credible source makes a claim of benefit. The skeptical reader is impressed.

The Los Angeles Times said the "The Pinchot Plan" has "long beaten the S&P 500," and to consider it if you are "looking for an investment that keeps growing, regardless of recessions or stock market turmoil."

Other mainstream news sources are also catching on. *The New York Times*, *The Wall Street Journal*, and *Barron's* have all reported on this opportunity in the last few months.

After more than a decade of working in the financial industry, I can tell you without hesitation that the "Pinchot Retirement Plan" is your best bet to make sure you don't run out of money.

For example...

3rd Promise — This one comes from the author of this letter.

You could have collected $63,934 in dividend payments over the last 2 years

Restatement of the 3rd promise in different words.

If you were participating in the "Pinchot Retirement Plan" over the past two years, you would have received 48 dividend checks during that time (that's about one every other week).

As I'll show you, these checks could have easily totaled $63,934 or more. That's an extra $2,664 per month.

8th Claim — This very specific claim ($63,934) is bigger than the first one ($18,850). That tends to increase credibility. The skeptical reader expects you to put the biggest claim first. Doing it this way seems low key and indicates that the author is believable.

9th Claim — This is a small claim (compounding interest), but it adds to the build-up.

4th (Indirect) Promise — There is an implied promise here, but it is a big one: The Pinchot Plan will "save" the prospect from a disastrous retirement.

10th Claim — This establishes the credibility of the man who invented the plan.

And what's remarkable about this plan is that at the same time, your assets grow every single day of the year—that's on top of your dividend payments!

I've put together a chart (to the right), which shows the "Pinchot Retirement Plan" payment schedule over the next 12 months.

But before I give you the details on how to get started, I'd like to show you exactly how this Plan works, so you can decide if it's something you want to consider.

Here's the full story...

The Man Who "Saved Retirement" for Americans

The "Pinchot Retirement Plan" is named after a long-time U.S. government employee (and former governor of Pennsylvania), named Gifford Pinchot.

If you've never heard of Pinchot, you're not alone.

He was an expert in the obscure but very lucrative profession of land management.

Mostly self-taught from a very young age—then schooled in France and Switzerland by geological and forestry scientists—Pinchot got his first big break when he was hired to manage George Vanderbilt's 7,000-acre Biltmore estate in North Carolina.

When Pinchot took over the property, it was a mess. Fires, clear-cutting, construction, and erosion had taken their toll. But Pinchot knew the rich natural resources (which included lumber, coal, and water) could provide profits indefinitely... if they were properly cared for.

Checks you'll receive in the next 12 months

By taking advantage of the Pinchot Retirement Plan, you should receive as many as 24 checks in the next year — about one every other week.

It's impossible to determine exactly when your checks will be delivered, but here's our estimated schedule for the next 12 months:

- Sept. 7th, 2007
- Sept. 9th, 2007
- Oct. 15th, 2007
- Nov. 13th, 2007
- Nov. 24th, 2007
- Nov. 29th, 2007
- Dec. 4th, 2007
- Dec. 8th, 2007
- Jan. 15th, 2008
- Feb. 11th, 2008
- Feb. 27th, 2008
- March 5th, 2008
- March 8th, 2008
- March 15th, 2008
- April 15th, 2008
- May 12th, 2008
- May 25th, 2008
- May 26th, 2008
- May 30th, 2008
- June 5th, 2008
- July 15th, 2008
- Aug. 11th, 2008
- Aug. 28th, 2008
- Aug. 30th, 2008

Keep in mind, the date you receive your first check depends on how soon you get started. In the last two years, these checks could have easily paid you an extra $63,934

Proof

Transition — This is paving the way to the proof contained in the sidebar. Putting some of your proof in sidebars is a great way to maintain the pace of the copy.

Qualifying Statement — See how the copywriter discloses the fact that these proofs are retroactively computed.

Proof — Presented in this way, the proof of monthly payments is very compelling.

Proof — This brief outline of Pinchot's career seems to prove out the claim that he was an expert in land management. Note the use of a famous historic person to substantiate the proof.

More Proof — This time, the proof is anecdotal, an account of what he did. In effect, a story.

Pinchot applied the scientific forestry techniques he learned overseas.

In short order, the Vanderbilt estate was making money for the first time ever. Vanderbilt was so impressed he set up an exhibit at the Chicago World's Fair to demonstrate Pinchot's model for land use.

In the past 2 years, "the Pinchot Plan" could have paid you $63,934 in dividends alone...

Restated Claim — This is the 3rd promise restated in different words.

The Vanderbilt story continues. It is dramatic. The reader feels like she is watching a movie. Stories — used as proof — carry a lot of emotional power.

Having established a reputation, Pinchot opened a New York office, to show wealthy Eastern landowners how to profit from their land. He made a fortune...

Pinchot bought a 148-foot, three-masted topsail schooner, complete with cabins and staterooms for a 12-man crew.

He and his family lived in a mansion called Grey Towers, in Milford, Pennsylvania. The property, which is now a National Historic Site, is a giant bluestone manor with three 60-foot turrets, 23 fireplaces, and 44 rooms.

Eventually, Pinchot's work—and his overwhelming success—attracted the attention of the U.S. Government.

Pinchot was hired by the Department by the Interior, then ran the Division of Forestry. In his first year, Pinchot instructed owners of more than 400,000 acres of private woodlands how to best care for and profit from their land.

In short, Pinchot devised laws and strategies that were good for the environment... and good for the economy. He helped many men get rich... and he made sure the natural resources would be around for generations to come.

But what does Pinchot's work have to do with you and your retirement?

It's a remarkable situation. Let me explain...

2nd Story — Having proven one claim with the Vanderbilt story, the copywriter introduces a 2nd story, this one in a different location. It, too, validates Pinchot's expertise and then leads to the U.S. government connection. Note: The 2nd story is half the length of the 1st. Why? Because it doesn't need to be as long. As the proofs pile up, the reader is more willing to accept increasingly shorter proofs.

What is the "Pinchot Retirement Plan" Exactly?

Today, there are 6 "Pinchot Plan" companies listed on the stock market. They follow the "Pinchot Model" for land use and development.

These operations, as you'll see, are not at all like regular businesses.

Transition — Having established Pinchot's impeccable credentials, the copy turns toward the reader (for the second time), addressing the benefits she will enjoy.

5th Promise — This promise is a curious one. It is a promise to explain how the plan will benefit the reader. This is a very direct promise. Eventually, all indirect leads must transition to direct promises. By taking the indirect approach, this is done after the reader has seen lots of proof and is now willing to believe what follows.

11th Claim — introduction of the USP of the plan

1st Proof of the 11th Claim

Instead, they simply manage tens of millions of acres of land. They sell timber, mining rights, manufactured products (like plywood and fiberboard), real estate (to developers and conservationists)... and rent their land to hunters, campers and farmers.

2nd Proof of the 11th Claim

Another thing that makes these Pinchot companies different from regular businesses is that, thanks to Sections 856-860 of the U.S. Internal Revenue Code of 1986, they pay no corporate taxes on the Federal level.

5th Promise — Additional benefit disclosed

As part of this arrangement, they are required to distribute 90% of their taxable income to shareholders.

3rd Proof of 11th Claim — Note: This is also a claim, but it acts as proof.

Yet another important difference between these operations and ordinary stocks is that they are not nearly as susceptible to the ups and downs of the economy as regular businesses.

12th Claim

If it's not a good time to sell land and timber, they simply wait. It's a luxury very few businesses have.

What's incredible is that these "Pinchot Plan" companies are a heck of a lot safer, and far more profitable, than ordinary stocks. (See the chart on the right.)

Let me show you one example of what I mean...

12th Claim Restated

Visual Proof — The comparative safety of the Pinchot Plan is quickly demonstrated by this graphic.

"The Pinchot Plan" Beat Stocks and Bonds for the Past 33 years

— "The Pinchot Retirement Plan"
— International Stocks
— S&P 500 Stock Index
— U.S. Bonds

10,000%
9,000%
8,000%
7,000%
6,000%
5,000%
4,000%
3,000%
2,000%
1,000%

1972 1975 1978 1981 1984 1987 1990 1993 1996 1999 2002 2005

How some Americans turned $10,000 into nearly $1 million

About 20 years ago, a group of businessmen from Seattle established a land-management business, using the model Gifford Pinchot developed for George Vanderbilt and other wealthy East Coast families.

How "The Pinchot Plan" can pay for your retirement

My name is Dr. Steve Sjuggerud. It's a Norwegian name (pronounced "sugar-rude"), although I was born and raised in the United States.

I spent the first half of my investment career working at big Wall Street institutions.

Right out of college, I got a job as a stockbroker. I learned pretty quickly that a broker's main job isn't to help his clients make money... but to simply get more clients.

My next job was working for a global mutual fund. I was promoted to Vice President, in charge of running a $50 million international fund. It turns out this job involved a lot of sales too. I had to spend several hours each day trying to sell the fund to potential investors.

Then I worked for two different billion-dollar hedge funds, and earned my PhD in Finance. I learned a lot in these positions, but I realized the hedge fund world still meant a lot of schmoozing, selling, and meetings... the part of the investment business I want to avoid.

So about 5 years ago I left all that behind, and started True Wealth, my own private advisory for retirees and people who want to retire soon. In that short time, we've grown to become one of the top 3 investment letters in America. We have readers in more than 125 countries.

I think we've done so well because month after month, my goal is to simply show you safe and profitable investment strategies you won't hear about anywhere else.

I've been looking at what we call the Pinchot Retirement Plan very closely over the past few years. What I've found is that it is one of the safest and most lucrative investments in the world right now.

   If you are interested in getting the full details, I would like
   to send you, absolutely free, my full Research Report, called:
   The Pinchot Plan - A New Way to a Worry-Free Retirement.

This Research Report explains exactly how these investments work. It explains how and when you'll receive your dividend checks... how much you will collect... and most importantly, how to make these 6 investments right away through almost any regular broker.

You see, I believe most people take way too much risk when they invest their money. My goal is to show you much safer opportunities — where you can make a small fortune at the same time.

My passion is investment research... finding great investments no one else is talking about.

To find new and profitable ideas, I make more than a dozen research trips every year all over the world.

7th Promise — Again, notice how direct this is.

Author Introduction — By now the reader believes in the value of the Pinchot Plan and is probably interested in knowing more about the person who is writing this letter.

Note the "positioning." True Wealth is for "retirees and people who want to retire soon," the same market this letter hopes to reach.

13th Claim — This validates the quality of the newsletter, which is the product being sold. Note how late in the sales argument this is done. That is typical for an indirect lead.

Impressive "CV" gives credibility to the author.

The Offer — The offer is indirectly introduced by the promise of a free report on the Pinchot Plan, which, as it turns out, is not the product. The newsletter is!

14th Claim — Steve is a conservative advisor. Note how this is implied, not stated.

It should be pretty obvious that the above sales letter was successful. It had a strong, indirect lead, and then a very well structured sales argument that included at least seven promises (indirect and then direct), 14 claims, and many proofs.

Now let's look at how the promise, claims, and proof are orchestrated in the following letter for a Nightingale-Conant product: *The Phoenix Process ...*

Nightingale ❤ Conant

All NEW!

In just **ONE MINUTE** ...
you can correct health problems that have been plaguing you for years

In just **ONE MINUTE** ...
you can eliminate your fears and anxieties and achieve true inner peace

In just **ONE MINUTE** ...
you can begin actively attracting wealth, love, success, and more

In just **ONE MINUTE** ...
you can COMPLETELY TRANSFORM your life!

Dear Friend:

Have your past attempts to make changes in your life led you to believe that change is incredibly difficult ... that it involves time, struggle, even pain and suffering?

What if I told you that, on the contrary, you can make enormous progress toward the life changes that you want — that you can, in fact, *achieve* those changes — in an instant!

It may sound too simple. It may sound too good to be true. But if you can suspend your skepticism for just a moment, I'm going to share with you the details of a revolutionary 60-second process that thousands of people have successfully used to do

over, please

Headline — Here you have three small promises leading to one big one: You can completely change your life in just one minute!

Lead — Note: This lead is very direct.

Promise — Very strong, very direct.

Promise of quickness is quantified.

everything from stopping the progress of disease … to manifesting critically needed financial resources … to reversing depression permanently … and much more.

This process is guided by science and firmly grounded in clinically proven facts about how the mind can effect lasting change at the physical, emotional, psychological, and cellular levels.

Yet its roots trace back to fundamental tenets of the great Western spiritual tradition — which holds that there is a positive life-giving force flowing through the universe and that when we synchronize ourselves with this force, perfect health and happiness are the inevitable outcomes.

The beauty of this process lies in its simplicity and accessibility. In the middle of a busy day, right where you're standing, no matter what is happening around you, you will have the power to transform your physiology, your emotions, your state of mind, and more. WITHOUT elaborate rituals. WITHOUT long drawn-out therapies. WITHOUT visiting and revisiting painful experiences of your past. WITHOUT dangerous, side-effect-laden pharmaceuticals.

Before I tell you more about this process, let me introduce the person who developed it — a person whose ideas may have already impacted your life.

Dr. Gerald Epstein is a world-renowned pioneer in the field of guided imagery. He was one of the first prominent voices to promote the idea of using mental techniques to address and heal physical and emotional disturbances.

Thirty years ago, Dr. Epstein's ideas were considered positively groundbreaking. Today — thanks in large part to *his* research and writings — the concept of using the mind to help heal the body has gained widespread mainstream acceptance.

Yet no sooner had Dr. Epstein injected his revolutionary ideas into a skeptical health and wellness establishment, than he was moving on to even more exciting avenues of exploration.

Specifically, he wanted to know: Was it possible to achieve the end-benefits of guided imagery more quickly — even, perhaps, instantaneously?

After all, guided imagery is based on the idea that all of our thoughts and behaviors — conscious and subconscious, intentional and automatic — are governed by pictures in the mind. The faster one could change the pictures, he reasoned, the faster the outward changes would manifest.

The resulting research bore out his hypothesis and led him to develop a radical new personal transformation methodology that he called **The Phoenix Process.**

2

Lead (cont.)

Claim — This system is scientific.

Claim — This system is simple.

Sales Argument Begins

Note: The subject is introduced at the same time as the expert.

Proof — by credentializing the expert behind the product, the copywriter proves to the reader why she can trust what she's being told.

Claim — Another claim that is not proven. Again, it seems reasonable … sort of.

Claim — This claim is not proven, yet it seems reasonable … more or less.

Note how the copy shifts here …

The USP is now defined. This is a unique kind of guided imagery — new and exciting.

The secret to changing in 60 seconds or less

Big Promise Restated

The phoenix is a mythological bird who, the story goes, died in flames, and then rose again out of the ashes, born anew.

In the same way, the process that Dr. Epstein has created enables you to emerge from the frustrations, false starts, disappointments, and fears of your past, a newly self-empowered person. The same, and yet totally transformed.

Promise — Expressed through analogy.

The Phoenix Process works so WELL because it replaces the habitual patterns and core beliefs you use to cope with everyday challenges and experiences — essentially, your mind's "operating system" — with new and far more positive, more effective patterns and beliefs.

Claim — Another unproven one.

It works so QUICKLY because it circumvents all the mental and emotional clutter to get to those patterns and beliefs. In other words, you don't have to think about, analyze, or even understand the techniques in this process. All you have to do for them to work is USE them.

Claim — Another claim, and a sort of logical proof at the same time.

The Phoenix Process is composed of four distinct yet interrelated practices:

The first practice balances your sensations, feelings, thought processes, and physiology whenever a recurring disturbing situation or belief confronts you.

The second practice prevents the physical, emotional, and psychological fallout that results when you encounter life experiences that create fear, panic, worry, anxiety, hostility, envy, or any other kind of distressing state.

The third practice takes charge of the doubt and indecision that plagues you, inhibits your activity, paralyzes your actions, and stops you from moving forward in life.

The fourth practice allows you to reverse disturbances in your body, relationships, emotions, or any other area, by dissolving destructive beliefs and images and replacing them with healthful, positive ones.

Indirect Promises — Here we learn more about the process. These seem to be proofs, but they are really promises in disguise.

Each of the four practices has, at its center, a one-minute technique designed to bring about an instantaneous whole-self transformation. Together, they represent a revolutionary and evolutionary comprehensive path to physical, emotional, mental, and spiritual health and well-being — restoring your power to act in freedom and opening the way to true longevity.

3   (over, please)

Big Promise — Restated again, in more abstract terms

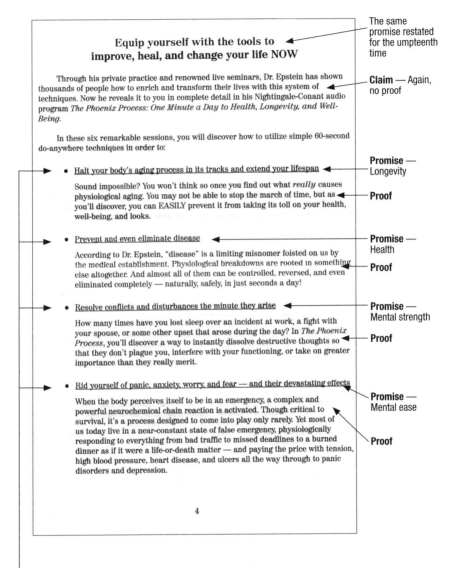

Equip yourself with the tools to improve, heal, and change your life NOW

> The same promise restated for the umpteenth time

Through his private practice and renowned live seminars, Dr. Epstein has shown thousands of people how to enrich and transform their lives with this system of techniques. Now he reveals it to you in complete detail in his Nightingale-Conant audio program *The Phoenix Process: One Minute a Day to Health, Longevity, and Well-Being.*

> **Claim** — Again, no proof

In these six remarkable sessions, you will discover how to utilize simple 60-second do-anywhere techniques in order to:

- Halt your body's aging process in its tracks and extend your lifespan

> **Promise** — Longevity

  Sound impossible? You won't think so once you find out what *really* causes physiological aging. You may not be able to stop the march of time, but as you'll discover, you can EASILY prevent it from taking its toll on your health, well-being, and looks.

> **Proof**

- Prevent and even eliminate disease

> **Promise** — Health

  According to Dr. Epstein, "disease" is a limiting misnomer foisted on us by the medical establishment. Physiological breakdowns are rooted in something else altogether. And almost all of them can be controlled, reversed, and even eliminated completely — naturally, safely, in just seconds a day!

> **Proof**

- Resolve conflicts and disturbances the minute they arise

> **Promise** — Mental strength

  How many times have you lost sleep over an incident at work, a fight with your spouse, or some other upset that arose during the day? In *The Phoenix Process*, you'll discover a way to instantly dissolve destructive thoughts so that they don't plague you, interfere with your functioning, or take on greater importance than they really merit.

> **Proof**

- Rid yourself of panic, anxiety, worry, and fear — and their devastating effects

> **Promise** — Mental ease

  When the body perceives itself to be in an emergency, a complex and powerful neurochemical chain reaction is activated. Though critical to survival, it's a process designed to come into play only rarely. Yet most of us today live in a near-constant state of false emergency, physiologically responding to everything from bad traffic to missed deadlines to a burned dinner as if it were a life-or-death matter — and paying the price with tension, high blood pressure, heart disease, and ulcers all the way through to panic disorders and depression.

> **Proof**

4

Indirect Promises — These bullets appear to be proofs, but are not. They are actually teasers. They provide the interested reader with a little bit of theory and the promise that she'll understand everything when she buys the product.

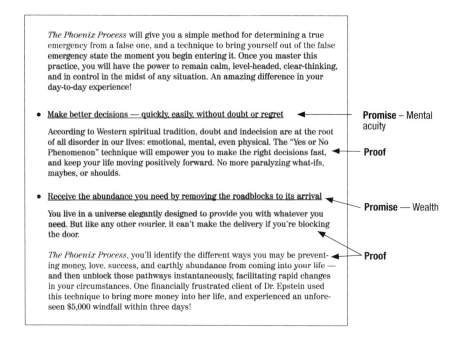

The Phoenix Process will give you a simple method for determining a true emergency from a false one, and a technique to bring yourself out of the false emergency state the moment you begin entering it. Once you master this practice, you will have the power to remain calm, level-headed, clear-thinking, and in control in the midst of any situation. An amazing difference in your day-to-day experience!

- Make better decisions — quickly, easily, without doubt or regret   **Promise** – Mental acuity

  According to Western spiritual tradition, doubt and indecision are at the root of all disorder in our lives: emotional, mental, even physical. The "Yes or No Phenomenon" technique will empower you to make the right decisions fast, **Proof** and keep your life moving positively forward. No more paralyzing what-ifs, maybes, or shoulds.

- Receive the abundance you need by removing the roadblocks to its arrival   **Promise** — Wealth

  You live in a universe elegantly designed to provide you with whatever you need. But like any other courier, it can't make the delivery if you're blocking the door.

  The Phoenix Process, you'll identify the different ways you may be prevent-   **Proof** ing money, love, success, and earthly abundance from coming into your life — and then unblock those pathways instantaneously, facilitating rapid changes in your circumstances. One financially frustrated client of Dr. Epstein used this technique to bring more money into her life, and experienced an unforeseen $5,000 windfall within three days!

The Seduction Is Going Perfectly ...

You found the right lady. You made the right moves. Hours went by like minutes in the living room. She feels like she has known you all her life.

And it's not just the fire that is burning in her heart. It is all the little confirmations that your living room conversation gave her: the questions you answered, the trophies you showed her, the many wonderful things you both agreed you'd love to do together.

And so the moment has arrived. You take her by the hand and lead her upstairs.

5

Upstairs in the Bedroom: The Close

The Three P's of the Close

- **Purpose:** to get rid of any residual skepticism or fear the prospect has so she will respond to the offer

- **Problem:** to convince the prospect to buy right then and there

- **Possibility:** to leave the prospect feeling delighted with her rational decision to buy

---

With every step up the stairs to the bedroom, you can feel her heart beating faster. You know that she is ready — that you could rip off her clothes the moment you get to the bedroom door.

But that's not what you are going to do. Because there is something you haven't told her.

Your house is designed perfectly for this seduction. At the top of the staircase, before you get to the master bedroom, there is an anteroom. It is furnished simply, with two chairs and a small table. But you have prepared it for this moment. Candles are on the table. Flowers are everywhere.

You light the candles and the room glows. The aroma from the flowers is intoxicating. You take her hand and look at her. She is flushed with anticipation.

The door between the anteroom and the bedroom is ajar. She glances through it to your bed. She seems ready to go there, but you ask her to sit down.

"There is one more thing I want you to know," you say.

She looks surprised. She sits. You see a flicker of curiosity in her eyes. You let her feel that curiosity for just a second, and then you say:

"I didn't say this before, because I don't think it matters. What we have together is what counts. This thing I'm going to tell you — well, it may surprise you. But I hope you'll agree that it shouldn't interfere with the relationship we can have ... the one we both want so much."

Now the curiosity in her eyes changes to fear. You can almost hear her thinking, "Oh, here it comes. Here is where he tells me that he's married or is divorced with six children or has herpes."

She swallows and asks, "What is it?"

"Well, the thing is," you start to say. (You are savoring the moment.) "Everything I've told you about me and what I've done and want to do is true. But ..."

"But?"

Her body language tells you she is ready for disappointment.

"But there is one more thing ..."

"What?!" She is practically screaming at you.

"Well, I happen to be ... I don't know how to say this delicately, but I happen to be ..."

"What is it?" She shouts.

It's just that ... I am about to become a very wealthy man."

"You what?"

"I'm about to become a multimillionaire." I hope it doesn't ruin what we have," you say. "I'm still the same person!"

You pause, enjoying the look on her face.

"The same person but with a few million in the bank?"

She leans her beautiful head back and shakes it, laughing.

"Are you upset?"

"No, no," she says, trying to control herself. She stands up, grabs your hand, and pulls you to the bedroom. "I think I can learn to live with it."

The False Close

In a direct-response sales letter, this is called the false close. It is where you add one additional, unexpected, and very powerful benefit at the end of the sales argument and before asking for payment. You can certainly finish off the sales letter without a false close. But used skillfully, it can solidify the sale in a very deep way.

The false close is used to surprise and delight the customer. She was emotionally hooked by the lead. She was rationally persuaded by the sales argument. Now she is ready to buy ... and would do so if you asked for the sale. But by being offered a new benefit at this point — something extra and unanticipated — she will feel very good about her decision to buy.

The false close has another benefit. It signals to the customer that the commercial relationship she has just begun will be one where she can expect to be surprised and delighted in the future. The false close is, therefore, a relationship-building tool that can have a positive effect on all future sales efforts to the customer.

The simplest way to introduce a false close is simply to say, at the end of the sales argument, "But wait ... there's more!" And often, that is the best way to do it. Sometimes, however, it makes more sense to stretch out the "but" part in order to create a little extra tension. That, in turn, will result in a bigger and more pleasant surprise when the second part ("there's more) is announced.

Take a look at this excerpt from a sales letter for *The Medical Investor* to see what I mean ...

> Before I give you the details... let me tell you about one more thing you'll receive with your subscription.
>
> It's the full details on what could easily be the most profitable stock in medicine...
>
> ## A Safe Way to Make 14,000%?
>
> Nearly 50% of Americans take prescription medication every single day – spending $200 BILLION each year to do so.
>
> Most people assume all that money is going to the Big Pharma giants that make the drugs. Not so.

At this point, the reader is sold. But, just to make sure, the copywriter adds something extra — a very strong promise of future

Here's another example of the false close — this one from a promo for AWAI's copywriting program ...

You can't miss it ... right there in BOLD letters.

> **But Wait. There's More.**
>
> When you enroll in my *Accelerated Program for Six-Figure Copywriting*, you'll also receive a free subscription to *Early to Rise*, a daily e-mail advisory from Michael Masterson on his secrets for achieving outrageous success in your business and personal goals.
>
> Among the topics you'll get in your *Early to Rise* e-mails:
>
> - How to get anything you want — by getting rid of the fear you have of being rejected.
> - How to always be "at the right place at the right time."
> - Why success is often a matter of making the right <u>small</u> decisions...and how to do that.
> - The 2 kinds of knowledge we make decisions on. Why you should listen to one and ignore the other.
> - The 3 most important questions in your life...and one good answer to each.
> - The two classic skills it takes to succeed at anything — and how to become a master of them.
>
> Regular *Early to Rise* subscribers pay $240 a year to receive the service. But a year's subscription is included FREE when you become a student in the *Accelerated Program for Six-Figure Copywriting*.

And here's an example from an online promo for *International Strategist* ...

> Six months should give you plenty of time to decide if you like my research and my investment philosophy. If you decide International Strategist is not for you, simply let me know by phone, mail, or e-mail, and we'll completely reimburse you for the entire subscription fee of $99.
>
> How much does *International Strategist* cost? And how can you get started?
>
> Before I give you the specifics, let me quickly tell you about one more investment idea I'm really thrilled about right now...
>
> "Graham's recommendations have helped me rake in over $100,000 in total gains. I made over 100% on two of his picks."
>
> ~Gerry Winston, Dayton, OH
>
> "I made 250% and 100% gains on two of your picks!!!"
>
> ~Hal Green
>
> "Your research has more than paid for itself. Keep up the good work."
>
> ~Manny Gabriel
>
> ## Canada's Best-Kept Retirement Secret
>
> As part of my travels, I uncovered another little-known way you can collect more retirement income...

Just as the writer seems to be on the verge of asking for the sale, he throws in one more piece of valuable information.

As I said, it is not necessary — or even desirable — to use a false close in every sales letter (just as it may not be necessary to stop in the anteroom before you and your lady love move on to the bedroom). But when you have an intuition that it might have a positive effect, give it a try.

The Close — the Completion of the Seduction

Most direct-response experts would agree that the main objective of the close is to seal the deal — to get the customer to complete the financial transaction. But master copywriters know there's more to it than that. Do it right, and you not only make the sale ... you also lay the groundwork for making many more sales to her in the future.

By the time you reach the close of the sales letter, you have gotten the prospect very excited about buying the product and you have convinced her that her excitement is rational. But you haven't yet disclosed all the specific terms of the sale. The payment options, the refund policy, and so on.

These last few details can cause trouble. The price, for example, may suddenly seem too high. Or the method of payment may seem cumbersome. Or the refund policy might seem weak in comparison to the price.

Any of these problems can thwart the sale, even though the customer wants to buy and is convinced that the purchase makes sense.

So now's the time to overcome that last shred of mental resistance and completely assure her that she's doing the right thing. One very effective way of doing that is to establish a high perceived value for the product — a value that's much higher than the price you're asking her to pay.

Transubstantiation or the
"Drop-in-the-Bucket" Technique

One way you can create a high perceived value for your product is to compare it to another similar product that has a much higher price. I used this technique more than 20 years ago with the original sales letter for The Oxford Club.

The Oxford Club was basically a financial newsletter — and, at the time, the established rate for a subscription to most financial newsletters was $100. (Curiously, that hasn't changed in all this time.) Rather than position the product as just another $100 newsletter, I persuaded my boss to invest some extra money so that it could operate as a club.

In the sales letter, I compared it to an English gentlemen's club. And then, at the close of the letter, I was able to discuss what such clubs actually charged their members. Something like this: "If you wanted to join the Suchandsuch Club in London, you would have to invest more than a thousand pounds a year ($1,500) to maintain your membership. As a charter member in The Oxford Club, your investment is only $100."

In his book *How to Overcome Price Resistance When Selling High-Priced Information Products*, Bob Bly explains another, similar technique. He calls it the "Drop-in-the-Bucket" technique, and describes it this way:

> *You want to show that the fee you charge is a drop-in-the-bucket compared to the value the product adds or the returns it generates. If your service helps buyers pass regulatory audits, talk about the costs of failing such an audit — fines, penalties, even facilities shutdowns. If your manual on energy efficiency in buildings cuts heating and cooling costs 10 to 20% a year, the reader with a $10,000 fuel bill for his commercial facility will save $1,000 to $2,000 this year and every year — more than justifying the $99 you are asking for the book.*

Here's an example of this technique ...

> True Wealth, by the way, costs just $199 for a full year of research and reports. Is it worth paying the equivalent of just $16 a month to learn about safe and profitable investment opportunities you'll hear about nowhere else? I think so, but here's what a few paid subscribers have told me recently...
>
> ** "I have been following Dr. Sjuggerud's investments for several years. Only wish I had known him early in my life. My $600,000.00 is now worth well over a $1,000,000.00. I think that I am almost ready to retire."
> – Clyde Lafond, 68, Burbank, CA
>
> ** "I have been reading Dr. Sjuggerud's reports for over six years. I took my wife's portfolio from her advisor and quadrupled it."
> – R. C. Beck, M.D., 80, retired cardiac surgeon
>
> ** "Of all the people I follow... Dr. Sjuggerud is, by far, the best at what he does...make me money! I have a 7-figure portfolio with many years of investing acumen. I'm up over 100K on his recommendations (in less than a year). No one comes close."
> – Raymond Martin, 53, former news producer at CBS
>
> The way I look at it, the longer you wait to get in on these investments, the less money you will have for retirement.

Here's another example, this time for a $345 information product on entrepreneurship ...

> Let me ask you – how much would you expect to pay someone to set you up in such a business – giving you the productivity tools you need such as...
> - a professional business plan, a proven marketing plan...
> - all the advertising materials you need, including a secret advertising technique **proven to work time after time in any market, for any product**...
> - teaching you every skill you need to be a top-notch, highly sought after professional in your field...
> - showing you how to practically guarantee success for your clients every time...
>
> and step-by-step instructions to operate and profit on an international basis?
>
> To gather all the tools and hire the professionals you would need... you could easily end up spending somewhere between $149,000 and $397,000 gathering the tools you need to set up a business that could generate the kind of income I showed you earlier.
>
> Obviously, you don't want to pay $149,000 or $50,000, or even $12,000 for **The Business Builder's Toolkit**. Don't worry, you won't even pay $10,000 – or even $5,000, although you must agree, if this enables you to make $88,975 per year... in your spare time... almost instantly... it's certainly worth that and more.
>
> That's why I think you'll be shocked to learn that **The Business Builder's Toolkit** sells for just $345.

Totaling the Values

I used another technique to create high perceived value for The Oxford Club. Instead of offering only a one- or two-year subscription, like the competition was doing, I took a hint from the English clubs we were imitating and offered a lifetime membership. In addition to a lifetime's worth of Oxford Club services and newsletters, this offer included a panoply of additional services and products, each of which was described and assigned a dollar value. I was then able to come up with a final "estimated retail value" for the lifetime offer that was worth more than 10 times the fee we were asking.

And to drive the point home, I tabulated the value "out loud" on the customer's behalf, making the arithmetic idiot proof.

Today, this technique is used so commonly that it is almost a cliché.

Here's an example ...

Masterclass – Bonuses
(this list will just grow and grow)

Masterclass – Bonus #1. *(currently sells for $4,397.00)*
The Advertising Masterclass on DVD / CD FREE! Over 20
hours of grade A advertising / copywriting information from
Alan Forrest Smith & Brett Mc Fall from January 2005
Advertising Masterclass.

Masterclass – Bonus #2. *(Value $397.00)*
Alan Forrest Smith Interview Series.

4 Private and compelling interviews with Alan revealing
gold-like information that you can apply within minutes to
your own business.

Masterclass – Bonus #3. *(Value $197.00)*
DVD of Front Page talk and demonstration from the World
Internet Summit UK 2005.

Masterclass – Bonus #4. *(Value $197.00)*
DVD of Alan Forrest Smith talking live at the World
Internet Summit UK about the importance of branding in
ANY business but especially on the web.

Masterclass – Bonus #5. *(Value $4,000.00)*
A $4,000 Voucher to use against any future Masterclass in
The Masterclass series. Next ones are in London, Australia
and France.

Masterclass – Bonus #6. *(Value $197.00)*
Marketing ESP Course – The perfect 3 step formula to
miraculous marketing results.

Masterclass – Bonus #7. *(Value $497.00)*
3 CD Pack – covering turning words into wealth, joint
ventures, mailing secrets, copy books DVD – 1 Hour
presentation on the ESP formula and the 12 step business
blueprint Entrepreneurial Spirits – The $10 Billion Dollar
book.

Masterclass – Bonus #8. *(Value $497.00)*
Ticket to the World Internet Summit USA Los Angeles
Sept 15th – 19th at 50% off the normal price

Masterclass – Bonus #9. *(at least Value $70,000)*

The Liquidating Bonus

There is one final technique you can use to create high perceived value. (Another one invented for The Oxford Club.) This
technique has come to be known as the liquidating bonus.

The idea here is that you first establish that the price the customer is about to pay is just a "drop in the bucket" compared to the value she is getting. Then you offer an additional surprise bonus as part of the false close. And finally, you offer the customer a premium with a value that is equal to the price you are asking for the product itself.

The Oxford Club lifetime offer had a sales price of $700. After establishing that the total value of the offer was in excess of $7,000 — making the $700 a fraction of what the customer might expect to pay — we threw in a set of leather luggage with a retail value of $700.

Most marketing experts will tell you that the bonuses you offer should be consistent with the products you are selling. So since, with The Oxford Club, I was selling information (basically, a newsletter subscription), conventional wisdom would say I should have given an additional information-based bonus, rather than a tangible bonus like luggage. But since I had already given away $7,000 worth of information, I thought adding an extra $700 worth of the same thing wouldn't be exciting. So we offered something that had an established retail value.

The prospective subscriber could say to himself, "Gee. This is a no-brainer. I invest $700 and get $700 worth of luggage. Everything else — the $7,000 worth of information and advice — I'm actually getting for free!" And to make the deal even more attractive, subscribers could keep the luggage even if they cancelled their membership.

As a general rule, I am in favor of giving away bonuses that are consistent with the products they are associated with. But with the liquidating bonus, I like the idea of giving something tangible that has an indisputable retail value.

When I wrote that first liquidating bonus for The Oxford Club, it was possible to get a set of leather luggage (imported from China) that could legitimately carry a $700 price tag but at a fraction of the retail value. Finding a deal like that isn't easy these days — but there's a lot you can do if you shop around for remainders and distress sales.

Like the false close, the liquidating bonus is not something you use all the time. But when you can use it, do so. It is very powerful.

Final Details

You cannot finish a sales letter without telling your prospect about her ordering options. And when you spell out the terms, there's a possibility that you will raise some new questions in her mind — questions that have not been addressed (or have not been fully addressed) in the sales argument.

So state the terms clearly, completely, and concisely — making sure the tone is consistent with the previous copy you've written.

Many copywriters change their "voice" dramatically when it comes to this mundane part of the sales letter, thinking, perhaps, that this is the "official" part of the transaction so it needs to be done in a lawyerly way. That's a mistake. The tone of voice in the close should be the same as it was in the headline, lead, and sales argument. Emotional consistency is the goal.

6

The House of Persuasion

You have structured the perfect sales letter — ending with a powerful close that firmly establishes the long-term beneficial business relationship you started when you wrote that opening line.

By identifying and tapping into your prospect's core emotional complex from the very beginning, you have achieved your goal.

The core complex is the cluster of feelings, thoughts, and desires she has when she encounters your sales letter. If she is a loan officer for a bank, for example, and the product you are selling is a manual on how to set up loans, your first job is to figure out what a loan officer might believe or feel about the job of setting up loans.

Does she believe successful loan officers need to be mentally tough ... or detail-oriented ... or emotionally persuasive? Is she worried about rising interest rates or increasing government regulations? Might she be frustrated by the legal requirements she is forced to work her way through? What does she want for herself? What does she need on an emotional level?

Before you write a single word of your sales letter, you should consider these questions and find something — some story or secret or prediction or promise — that encapsulates your answer to them. You must discover the feelings, thoughts, and desires that are running around inside your prospect's head and heart. Once you get hold of that story, secret, prediction, or promise, make it the cornerstone of your teaser, your headline, and your lead.

Your prospect's core complex should serve as the foundation of the sales letter, the deeply laid, concrete base on which you can build your house of persuasion.

To review the key steps:

1. Begin with a teaser for the envelope that encapsulates the prospect's core emotional complex.

2. Make sure the look of the envelope is consistent with that core feeling.

3. Replicate the teaser as a headline or create a new one — a "big promise" that dovetails with the teaser.

4. Make sure the package contents — the paper stock, typefaces, color selections, etc. — do not contradict the feeling conveyed by the headline.

5. Write a lead that immediately engages the prospect at a gut level and (in the space of a few hundred words) gets her thinking, "This is really good! I'm glad I'm reading this."

6. Build on that lead in the sales argument by making more promises and claims and proving them. Use every technique at your disposal — historical anecdotes, fictionalized stories, scientific studies, customer surveys, testimonials, etc. — to rationalize the offer. Make it coherent, sensible, and logically persuasive.

7. Close the letter with an unexpected extra benefit to make the prospect feel good about her decision to buy.

8. Before signing off, make sure every possible question has been answered and every possible objection has been addressed.

The Beginning of a Beautiful Relationship

When you were first challenged to find and seduce a woman in a single evening, you probably thought, "This is crazy! I can't do that!"

But by taking the right steps — both at the Explorers Society party and at your house — you succeeded. Looking back at it now, it almost seems too easy.

And that's how you will feel about writing breakthrough sales letters if you follow the suggestions made in this book. It may seem daunting at the outset, but when you take the process one step at a time, you can write one great sales letter after another!